PIRENE'S FOUNTAIN

Pirene's Fountain

Senior Editor	Lark Vernon Timmons
Editors	Elizabeth Nichols
	Mark McKay
Managing Editor	Steve Asmussen
Associate Editors	Royce Hamel
	Linda Kim
	Paul Kim
	Kelly Cressio-Moeller
Web Design & Layout	Katherine Herschler
Art Consultant	Tracy McQueen
Publisher & Editor	Ami Kaye

Pirene's Fountain

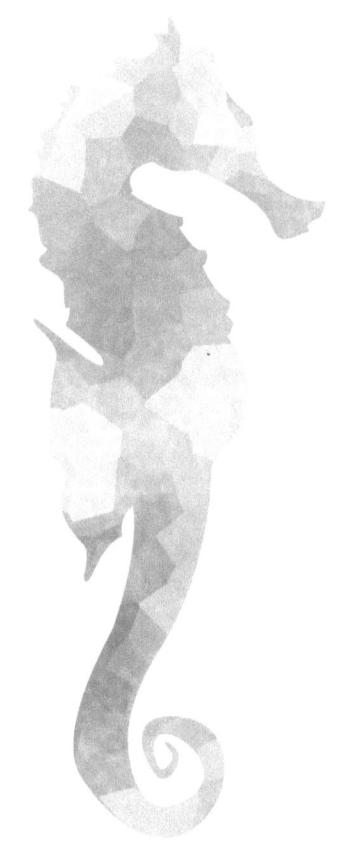

Volume 8, Issue 16

 Pirene's Fountain: A Journal of Poetry
Volume 8, Issue 16
Copyright © 2015 Pirene's Fountain
Paperback ISSN 2331-1096

Layout, Book & Cover Design: Steven Asmussen
Copyediting: Elizabeth Nichols & Linda Kim
Cover Artist: Tracy McQueen

All rights reserved: except for the purpose of quoting brief passages for review, no part of this book may be reproduced or transmitted in any form or by any means, electronic or mechanical, including photocopying, recording, or by any information storage and retrieval system, without permission in writing from the publisher.

Glass Lyre Press, LLC
P.O. Box 2693
Glenview, IL 60025

www.GlassLyrePress.com

Winter, 2015-16

Dear Readers,

Welcome all to the 2015 *Pirene's Fountain* annual print edition! We are ever-mindful of our loyal readership and valued contributors and extend our sincere thanks for their continued support. For those who are discovering our poetry journal for the first time, we invite you to peruse and enjoy— it would be an honor to have you return to *PF*'s pages.

Plans are currently in the works for a modified online version of *Pirene's Fountain* to be offered with future print editions. Please visit GlassLyrePress.com and PirenesFountain.com for ordering information and submission guidelines. In addition, be advised ad space is available to interested parties.

As with our first print edition's cover and design concept, the seahorse image is the creative vision and collaborative effort of Tracy McQueen and Steve Asmussen. Also in this issue, besides a record number of reviews, we are honored to showcase and interview two multi-talented and highly respected poets, Allison Joseph and Lois P. Jones, and present a craft interview/featurette with Jane Hirshfield.

On behalf of all our staff, I would like to congratulate this year's Pushcart and Liakoura nominees, especially the winner of the Liakoura Prize, Ken Meisel. Congratulations also to Joan Colby, the 2015 Kithara winner, and Megan Merchant, the 2015 Lyrebird winner.

Looking ahead, our stunning *Silk & Spice* anthology (PF 17) will feature poets Joseph Fasano and Vandana Khanna. We are planning a new issue for 2017 called *Skin Deep* and will post guidelines when we are ready.

In closing, valued newcomers, loyal readers, writers, artists all, we invite you to immerse yourselves in our latest *PF* issue with the hope that you will be inspired—and your time spent be rewarding and memorable.

Lark Vernon Timmons
Senior Editor
Pirene's Fountain

Pirene's Fountain News & Events

Earlier this year, Michael Fisher interviewed Ami Kaye for *The Review Review* with a focus on *Pirene's Fountain*, which launched its first online issue in January 2008. It is hard to believe *PF* will be celebrating its tenth anniversary in a couple of years! We decided to do something special to mark the occasion, and are reading submissions for *Collateral Damage*: an anthology to benefit disadvantaged children all over the world.

Andrea Witzke Slot at the POETRY Foundation

We had a chance to attend the POETRY Foundation open doors event where four superb poets, including Andrea Witzke Slot, read their work. The Glass Lyre staff attended Ruth Goring's beautiful book launch for *Soap is Political*, where she was accompanied by guitarist Nelson Sosa. We also went to the *RHINO* release party graciously hosted by Ralph Hamilton. Later in Spring, we attended the Poets & Writers event in Chicago, and we had the pleasure of seeing Dana Gioia at the Cindy Pritzker auditorium, as well.

Steve Asmussen and the Glass Lyre staff put together a fabulous showing at Printer's Row Literary Festival 2015 here in Chicago! They met the local literati, made some new friends, and sold a number of books, including copies of the first print issue of *Pirene's Fountain*.

Associate Editor, Paul Kim, mans our Printer's Row Lit Fest table.

On September 26th, we once again celebrated the 100 Thousand Poets for Change global event once again at our annual Live Lyre reading event. Elizabeth Nichols welcomed our readers and spoke about worldwide peace and sustainability. The featured poets who read their gorgeous work included Joan Colby, Ruth Goring, Ralph Hamilton, Sandra Marchetti, Marc Frazier, Helen Degen Cohen, Bill Yarrow, Angela Narciso Torres, and Lois P. Jones, who flew in from California for the event. Sara Henning, Pam Miller, and Kevin Bradshaw read their excellent poems during open mic, which was led by Royce Hamel.

This year we started a new folio series called *Aeolian Harp*. Ralph Hamilton was the co-editor for our debut issue, and Volume Two will be co-edited by Lois P. Jones.

Pirene's Fountain has completed readings for next year's new issue: an anthology called *Silk & Spice* that will be released next year. We are working on a new project for 2017 called *Skin Deep* that explores our perception of beauty and its impact on our life choices and decisions. We will be posting guidelines for this themed issue soon.

In response to recent terror attacks in Paris, Beirut, and around the world, we are also putting together a "World Peace Anthology" to raise funds and awareness. We are fortunate to have the formidable talents of Diane Frank, Lois P. Jones, Rustin Larson, Gloria Mindock, and Melissa Studdard for this project.

In recent news, we were deeply saddened to hear that Helen Degen Cohen, co-founder of *RHINO*, passed away. We are grateful to have known her and to have had her as a featured reader at our events. She was very supportive of Glass Lyre Press and a beacon for the literary community at large.

Helen Degen Cohen at Live Lyre 2015
Photo: Bill Yarrow

Pushcart Prize Nominations

Pirene's Fountain is pleased to nominate the following poems for the Pushcart Prize:

"The Hand that Left the Puppet Grasping" — **Jim Pascual Agustin**
"Public Radio" — **Patricia Caspers**
"Visiting my Mother in Montreal" — **Hedy Habra**
"Stonehenge" — **Richard Krawiec**
"Cleave" — **M. Nasorri Pavone**
"When a Person Carries Darkness Inside" — **Martin Willits Jr.**

We thank all our nominees for sharing their very fine work with us and wish them the best of luck!

2015 Liakoura Prize

Pirene's Fountain awards the Liakoura Prize to a poet with exceptional and impactful work. Poems are selected from the current issue by the *Pirene's Fountain* team of editors, and then sent blind to an outside editor who then chooses the winner.

Liakoura is the modern name of Mount Parnasssus, the home of the muses in Greece. Specifically, Liakoura is where the mythical Pirene's fountain is located near Delphi. Due to its proximity to the wellspring of the muses, Liakoura is also broadly defined as a collection of poetry, the world of poetry and/or poets, or any active poetic or artistic space.

The Pirene's Fountain editors nominated the following poems for the 2015 Liakoura Prize Award:

"Your Reflection"—**Julie Brooks Barbour**
"Parting Words"—**Jeremy Cantor**
"Three Tips for Inhabiting Our Material World"—**Karen Craigo**
"That Day the Sky Was Stone"—**Gail Goepfert**
"Watching Bilal Fall"—**Ken Meisel**
"Poe Pound Villanelle"—**Bill Yarrow**

This year's winner was selected by Tony Barnstone. Tony Barnstone is the Chair of English at Whittier College and author of 18 books, a chapbook of poems, and a music CD, *Tokyo's Burning: WWII Songs*, based on interviews with WWII veterans and their families by Barnstone and others.

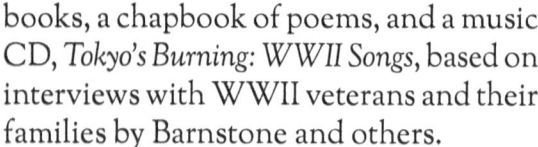

His poetry books include *Pulp Sonnets* (Tupelo Press); *Beast in the Apartment* (Sheep Meadow Press); *Tongue of War: From Pearl Harbor to Nagasaki* (BKMK Press); *The Golem of Los Angeles* (Red Hen Press); *Sad Jazz: Sonnets* (Sheep Meadow Press); *Impure* (Univ Press of Florida); and selected poems in Spanish, *Buda en Llamas: Antología Poética* (1999-2012).

He is co-editor of the anthologies *Poems Dead and Undead* and *Monster Poems: Human and Inhuman Monster Poems* (both from Everyman Pocket Poet Editions). He is also the editor of several world literature textbooks.

Barnstone's books of translation include *Chinese Erotic Poems* (Everyman Press), *The Anchor Book of Chinese Poetry* (Anchor Books), *The Art of Writing: Teachings of the Chinese Masters* (Shambhala Publications, Inc.), *Out of the Howling Storm: The New Chinese Poetry* (Wesleyan University Press), *Laughing Lost in the Mountains: Selected Poems of Wang Wei* (University Press of New England), and *River Merchant's Wife* by Ming Di (translated from the Chinese by Tony Barnstone, Neil Aitken, Afaa Weaver, Katie Farris & Sylvia Burn with the author, Marick Press).

Fellowships include: the NEA, NEH Summer Stipend, and the California Arts Council. Selected awards: Poets Prize, Pushcart Prize, Grand Prize of the Strokestown International Poetry Festival, John Ciardi Prize in Poetry, and the Benjamin Saltman Prize in Poetry.

Barnstone was raised in Indiana and lived for years in Greece, Spain, Kenya, and China. He earned his B.A. in English and Spanish Literature at U.C. Santa Cruz and he earned an M.A. in Creative Writing and a Ph.D. in English Literature at U.C. Berkeley.

Pirene's Fountain
Presents the 2015 Liakoura Prize winner:

Ken Meisel
for
"Watching Bilal Fall"

The poem can be found on page 75 of this issue.

Contents

Poetry

Jim Pascual Agustin
    The Hand that Left the Puppet Gasping   23

R. Steve Benson
    Geographies   24

George Bishop
    Remembering My Aunt   25
    Shelling   26

Karina Borowicz
    Fallen   27

Anne Britting Oleson
    Anti-Sonnet   28

Julie Brooks Barbour
    The Room of Ornaments   29
    Your Reflection   30

Jody Burke-Kaiser
    The Things That Stay   31
    Valentine   32

Jeremy Cantor
    Parting Words   34

Patricia Caspers
    Public Radio   35

Karen Craigo
    Three Tips for Inhabiting Our   36
        Material World

Rachel Dacus
    False Star   38
    The Camel's Teeth   39

Val Dering Rojas
    Conchology   40

Dennis Etzel Jr.
   From the highest point overlooking   41
   This forest sanctuary   42

Patricia Fargnoli
   Eastern Dobsonfly   43

Ruth Foley
   For a while everything tastes the same   44
   The end of the world begins   45
   Why Not   47

Trina Gaynon
   In Paradise   48
   Sleep Study   49

Gail Goepfert
   That Day the Sky was Stone   50

Hedy Habra
   Heartbeat   51
   Once Upon a Time, an Olive Tree   52

Taylor Hamann
   estate sale   54

A.J. Huffman
   Devouring Silence   55

Lois P. Jones
   Exhumation   56

Allison Joseph
   Self-Portrait As Ice Cream Truck   57
   To Know a Poet   59

Alan S. Kleiman
   Dew Etc.   61

Laurie Kolp
   Temptation, Passed   62

Richard Krawiec
   Stonehenge   64

Rustin Larson
    Aphrodite and the Gods of Love   65
    Dreams   66

Sean Lause
    Homecoming   68

Helen Losse
    Hospitalized in December   70

Ken Meisel
    Medicine Circle   72
    Watching Bilal Fall   75

Corey Mesler
    Monsters from the Id   79
    My body asks   80

Naila Moreira
    Lines from Base Camp   81

M. Nasorri Pavone
    Cleave   82

Jonathan K. Rice
    Girl Flying A Kite   83

Judith Skillman
    Desire   84
    Queen Anne's Lace   85

Joannie Stangeland
    This Shade So Early Clings   87

Annie Stenzel
    Chiding the Muse   88

Maria Terrone
    Dreams & Dismemberment   89

Donna Vorreyer
    Provisions   91

Martin Willits Jr.
    When a Person Carries Darkness Inside   92

Nancy Wilson
   Taste the Wind   93
   Wednesday   94

Sarah Ann Winn
   Housewarming the Last House on Holland Island, Fallen into the Bay   95

Bill Yarrow
   Maurice Utrillo: Portraitist of Street and Sky   97
   Poe Pound Villanelle   98
   Spontaneous Tranquility   99
   When We Marry: A Poem in Two Voices   100

Showcases: Lois P. Jones and Allison Joseph

Lois P. Jones: Poet, Photographer, and Radio Host Incomparable   103
In Conversation with Poet and Radio Host Lois P. Jones   110
Alison Joseph: Rooted in Rhythm   119
In Conversation with Allison Joseph   129

Featurette: Jane Hirshfield

Jane Hirshfield's Ten Windows: How Great Poems Transform the World   135
The Beauty by Jane Hirshfield   136
In Conversation with Jane Hirshfield   138

Reviews

Strange Theater by John Amen   152
Love is a Burning Building by J.P. Dancing Bear   156

Temporary Champions	159
by Darren C. Demaree	
Dreaming of Rain in Brooklyn	162
by Howard Faerstein	
Numinous	167
by Leila Fortier	
Paradise Drive	172
by Rebecca Foust	
Teaching a Man to Unstick His Tail	176
by Ralph Hamilton	
How to be Another	180
by Susan Lewis	
State of the Union	182
by Susan Lewis	
This Visit	184
by Susan Lewis	
Femme Eterna	186
by Lyn Lifshin	
Brash Ice	188
by Djelloul Marbrook	
The Lifeline Trembles	191
by Mary Kay Rummel	
The Greenhouse	194
by Lisa Gluskin Stonestreet	
I Ate the Cosmos for Breakfast	198
by Melissa Studdard	
Blood Flower	202
by Pamela Uschuk	
Publication Credits	207
Contributor Notes	210
Advertisements	223

Then in these swelling and ebbing currents,

these deepening tides moving out, returning,

I will sing you as no one ever has,

streaming through widening channels

into the open sea.

—Rainer Maria Rilke

From: "The Book of a Monastic Life"
Rilke's Book of Hours (Riverhead Books, 2005)
(Translated by Barrows & Macy)

POETRY

The Hand that Left the Puppet Gasping

Jim Pascual Agustin

That moment when oxygen
made a final escape from your lips
marked a new chapter of myth
making. Fortified walls rose

not where it was forbidden to build
a shrine, but in an imagined world
by those left behind. To silence
a thought with a bullet is to admit

defeat. A lesson never learned.
Osama, you are now open country.
Whoever claims to tell your story will paint
a portrait of their own fears, believe

what they choose. I could almost
hear you laughing underwater
as you caress your beard. Laughter
so loud the fish can't sleep.

Geographies

R. Steve Benson

Fallen from parent
pines cones
resemble
tiny temples
with tiers
of balconies
always open
in the sifted dust.

Remembering My Aunt

George Bishop

Always the face of something gone
wrong, words like *hopeless and futile*
inadequate as an angel on a dead tree.
Our family used to gather for dinner
each Christmas until her husband fell
dead in the driveway one snowy night.
I remember bringing my first camera

to the final meal, Santa's last good idea.
I still have the black and white somewhere,
everyone at the table except me, the only
one alive now, eating at Bruno's alone.
I remember the cheap flash going off that
Christmas, little lights dancing as they
faded in everyone's eyes but mine.

Shelling

for Chris

George Bishop

Oyster beds bearing no resemblance
to anything desirable, where I'd love
to nap, dream or die. The abandon
of pelicans and ruin of shells wearing
away in every wave. Everything
pieced, worn, hidden, regret growing
just below the skin of an old man
nose to nose with another old man,

telling him off, telling it like it is—

maybe the chiseled frowns of women
tobacco-bound, carved into mirrors
that mistake them for the dark cracks
in a wall they can't detect. Whatever
it is I'm looking for, this is as close
as I can come—a colander of shells
soaking in dish soap and warm water,
the inside of emptiness coming clean.

Fallen

Karina Borowicz

A bad year for acorns. For the second year
in a row, the oaks didn't drop any.
There were storms and they all lost limbs.
They're still trying to recover.

Snow is a creature of contrasts.
It's very stubborn, even the first gentle snowfall
shaken from the warm underside
of an enormous wing.

Winter twilight blue, sobbing indigo.
Blue heartbeat, bolt of violence. Blue
out of which I've fallen.

Anti-Sonnet

Anne Britting Oleson

I'd write you *Sonnets from the Portuguese*
but for one insurmountable problem
or two; among them, first, is having no
Portuguese blood to make its way through these
veins: only the fiery sense of singing
just beneath my skin, the sonnets and songs
both formal and free, full melody lines
building in volume from the one longing
where your fingers played an adagio.
I can hear the hum of my mongrel blood,
its brash and wordless voice below all thought:
music with its insistent crescendo
for you—a low siren's song—intensely.
This is its poem. You are its harmony.

The Room of Ornaments

Julie Brooks Barbour

You stand on wall-to-wall red carpet
in the center of a large room, ornaments

on every wall. Gold sconces. A family crest.
Two crystal chandeliers hang from the ceiling.

Faces you recognize, the makers of rules,
stare from red walls. You are the only person

in the room. You were told to wait,
so you stand still as if lack of motion

will force a voice to tell you to move.
When you were a child, your mother

would not let you attend a large party
held in her honor. You remember

the fanfare in the street below your window
and being confined to a room with an aunt

who would not let you leave. Here you are again,
waiting for someone to open a door.

Your body casts two shadows,
one for the present and one for the past

from which you cannot remove yourself.

Your Reflection

Julie Brooks Barbour

It is only a sheet of glass, cut to meet a frame.
What you see is really behind the glass,

in the silver coating: streaks of gray
spiral into your curls and a whisper of dark hair

rests above your lips. The creases of your smile
no longer fade quickly. You are not elastic—

you are etched by lines and marks, a pattern of age.
Bad luck descends if you rebel and strike back,

if you smash your reflection to shards,
but this mirror is only an object.

It holds images as they pass: a girl's dark hair,
her head turned toward the opposite wall.

The Things That Stay

Jody Burke-Kaiser

They found a mammoth tusk below a parking lot in Seattle.
Twenty-two thousand years old, older than any cup,
leather lace, or stone tool. Badly waterlogged,
each pocket of bone holding its own little drop,
afloat in the soil.

We have parked our hybrid SUV's full of hockey equipment,
overdue library books, snack crackers made of indigestible
wood pulp over it, filled our trunks with wine and boys
and played our music so loud the dead calcium caves
of each cell must have echoed,
hummed beneath us.

Still, it is a lost tooth for fairies to find,
tucked beneath, fragile as a small boy's hand,
heavy as belief.

The thing that stays is as brittle as a sea shell, as fluid as milk,
as hollow as a cave forming one drop at a time.
Steady as the exchange rate, money for bone,
money for the copper thrust of tongue in the gap left behind,
money for the joy of eating apples again
after weeks of worry.

My last child lost his first tooth, now they fall
like leaves. He is a gummy old man.
Twenty-two thousand years ago the last mammoth in Seattle
laid his old bones down and let go,
nerve and sinew and clutch snapped clean,
gave up his last weapon,
his only tool.

Valentine

Jody Burke-Kaiser

Hearts frighten me,
the way they explode in airports
as you drag your luggage uphill.
The way they keep
small boys waiting.
Four caves that collapse and rebuild,
collapse and rebuild,
like a film wound backwards.
Pushing for the exits.
Dead when they are at last
most open.
Dead when there is finally
room to grow.
Synchronized like the watches of spies,
always taking,
passing room to room,
arguing the right of return.
Skeptical red exchanges
of oxygen and trash.
A clock, a bomb, a bride
wed to a too small number.
My ear over your chest,
lifted and dropped by your heavy sleep.
I will not count,
forward or backward,
not pray or cross fingers and toes,
not pour salt in a ring around our bed,
not keep time,
fingers thrumming on taught sheets.
Nor will I sleep,
not once,
and regret the push

of your presence
against the bone of my cheek,
regret the number of open and closed
doors between us,
the chambers we hold empty,
or the pitchers we overfill.

Parting Words

Jeremy Cantor

My mother, fluent in four languages,
lost the only one we understood,
her English pinched out like a candle wick
by another blood clot in her head

Her French was still impeccable,
the nurse from Cameroon informed us,
but we understood no French

I asked, in English, if she still knew German
She replied in German,
one more language
we did not understand

My mother's mother tongue, *mamishe loshen*,
was Yiddish, 'til the age of six, and so
we guessed that it would be the last to go

My brother found a neighbor who was fluent
By then she wasn't speaking
Her eyes
were closed

I wasn't with her at the end; I'd like to think
that as she went where nobody could follow,
she recognized as hers something familiar,
whether sense, or syllable, or sound,
in whatever it was the stranger said to her

Public Radio
For Ira

Tricia Caspers-Ross

At thirteen every day was a slow, hot, breath
released into a windless sky.
A smear of lip gloss, hippo tongue pink,
to distract from teeth already lost to the asphalt.

I stretched cotton white shorts over new hips
and flip-flopped to the gas station patio
where I swung my legs from a bench
in hopes that some traveling smoker
might offer me a Pepsi, a Kit Kat, or a ride.

I walked a rolling stretch of dead-end
roads and wondered about the faces
behind windshields,
whether they ate dinner together around a table,
whether they would know me.

When I should have been asleep,
I clicked on my birthday boom box, volume low,
and ballooned the empty shadows with sound.

Once I twisted the dial far into the desert
heard a pledge drive, and for the first time
felt the down-deep body thrill
of a man's rough voice in my ear,
in the dark, whispering *please*.

Three Tips for Inhabiting Our Material World

Karen Craigo

*A shelter made of dirt
is still a shelter.* My son
tells me this, calls it
a pro-tip, one
among dozens he spins
out of air. Later,
he'll sit on a red chair
and say *You may notice
this is a fake red chair,
like a fake milk pitcher
that can also be used
with root beer*—each tip
so like a sequin
I hold it in my fingers,
turn it to pan the light.
Some days he comes home
and the first thing he does
is pull from his pocket
a feather. He smuggles
these to me in secret,
like the code
to a lock, and I keep them
in a vase—glorious
tail feathers, pin feathers,
scraps from a wing.
He knows I love these
artifacts of flight or battle,
prismatic, pocket-bent
or frayed. Another tip:
*An ice cream truck
is not an ice-cream truck—
I mean it is not a truck*

made out of ice cream.
He is working on a notion
about refuge—about where
we may settle together,
and with what
we may line our nest.

False Star

Rachel Dacus

I rest after my night walk on a bench. Old bone,
soft rifts, blood bleached, I breast-stroke
the July dark, while Venus hangs
close as a porch light.

Windows across from the lot flicker
with red lanterns and Motown.
They rock behind the curtains
while the music revs like the Mustangs
zooming late down the street.

I hide in the corners of my eyes,
wanting to dance in the shadow
of this cricket-loud oak. Unable
to go home to my own life
and its diminishments, I'm switched on
in this fable of Friday night.

I watch the moon rise and flex
his round biceps and I bite
into that apricot flesh,

but when I hear footsteps
and a young face rounds
the corner, I flee. Shameless,
that false star, daring that way
to wink at me.

The Camel's Teeth

Rachel Dacus

I need more light just when
the suns slides offstage
and flickers on the eaves,
and a lighthouse's revolving flash
skewers the mist I carry home
on my sloping shoulders.

I always want what's slipping away.
Autumn's a procession of animals:
the camel leads, with his desert-cropping teeth,
then a roof rat pebbles into my dreams.
The small brown snake of rain
swishes between my toes.

Every night I contemplate the ceiling's
fine print and what I have left
of this year, then seek lap blankets, socks,
and pillows. I count the imps of ambient light,
remember to re-angle the blinds
to let in more sun.

I clutch at each spark, descend
into sleep as into my own internal glow
like a blind, deep sea fish
who navigates by bio-luminescence.
All night I can hear the stems rotting.

It's dark when I wake
but now the shuttered morning light
stripes the wall honey.
Though I am crunched in winter's teeth,
I rise and touch the glass door,
how in warmth it dreams kisses of snow.

Conchology

Val Dering Rojas

The shells in the chiffonier are glass islands. You closeted them using a sailor's system of making knots; opted for a cupboard as a way to shield your freckles from the sun; forgot the sound of unlatching. Each island: classification, diagnosis: (tiny) butterfly, (tiny) open heart, (tiny) skeleton. Blame the temblor for why the waves come in code: small-small-large-small-tsunami. The door opened, and an entire ecosystem surfaced: bivalves, gastropods, cephalopods, polyplacophora, tube sponge, algae bloom. And the carapace of an urchin, which is called a test. But this is not tribulation. This is not the sea leaving your veins. This is not a crucible of salt. This is the whelk prying open the oyster's shell. This is the crab taking the whelk. This is the albatross swallowing the crab. This is everything, feeding off of everything else.

From the highest point overlooking

Dennis Etzel Jr.

From the highest point overlooking the city's wonder, apology
stretched underneath the soil, a moth aching to be set free.
I sketch my profile on the monument, that water tank marker
marking shadows, demons set free out of mouths. Let's get real.
The graffiti warned us about weight, about toes in the soil.
I come up here to get away from the hold
Topeka thrusts, as if this place is separate, apart
like the thumb. Sure, drought followed that tornado,
you know the one if you're from here. If you're from here,
there will be a heaven, I'm sure. There will be weeping.

This forest sanctuary

Dennis Etzel Jr.

This forest sanctuary
slides underfoot, spreads
and twirls vines and roots
against the darkness
with episodes of depression,
nausea, forgetfulness.
Sometimes someone asks
for a book of one hundred
most beloved poems, or for
a one-night stand, while
I realize I was meant
for building garden plots,
that I'm the kind that cruises
streets for not the road, but
the ruins, houses that housed
those who hated
my mothers, lesbians living
in the neighborhood, green
sprouting up to paint itself
an opera's last act, purple
hints spiking that Kansas City
Jazz, and whatever swing
I jumped out of landed me
in Roman coliseums, amusements
to dog walkers who chose
not to scoop up poop. Thanks,
I forgot all about that, as the hail
falls with cold rain, and if you
think me greedy or arrogant, I will
bake those chicken enchiladas
for the grandmothers inside you.

Eastern Dobsonfly

Patricia Fargnoli

Mid-July, my arms laden with groceries,
I am struggling to open the screen door when I see him:
five inches of fly if you count his antennae,
which cross over each other like a pair of sickles.
He doesn't move when I open the door,
doesn't move when I bend close to examine
the veined four-inch wings,
their gray latticed lacework folded along
his body, his beastly head, the mandibles
made not for eating but for
clutching the female.
I learn he has come from the nearby brook,
and has lived in all three worlds—
water, earth, air—
three years in water as larva
for which we have many names:
hellgrammites, grampus, crawlerbottoms, go-devils,
then three weeks as pupa on land hidden under rocks.
until his last transubstantiation here so briefly in the air.
He has no need to eat, only to find a mate
and clutch her and multiply.
Corydalus cornutes Linnaeus named him—
"noun meaning a form of bogey or a haunting spirit."
This is the second year
such a creature has alit on my door
same month of the year, in exactly the same spot.
He has only three days to live.
I will wear his likeness in a necklace of silver.

For a while everything tastes the same

Ruth Foley

The sea stone I hold in my mouth my tongue the soft
tissue between index finger and thumb a sudden breath
of wind following a truck under a bridge with just
enough clearance the breath held in the cab the hair
of the dog that licked my hand awake beneath
the covers the covers themselves the air that's not enough
to feed me coming as it does from between your teeth
my teeth some kind of dinner with some kind of wine
the winter morning we walked the dogs across
the lake the way the fish held somewhere below
and what of your lumberjack arms the rain freezing
in your beard the smoke from the fire we built later.

The end of the world begins

Ruth Foley

as we knew it would, in the library,
where a volunteer is rolling a cart
through the stacks, coughing into
his hand, then shelving books. He

has made it through mysteries and
into science fiction, and the woman
who trails behind him looking for
something she hasn't yet read will

pick up a novel, read the flap, put
it back, and end up checking out
something she first read years ago
and won't finish this time. On her way

home, she will stop at the store,
choose some plums by feel. She
will need to feel a lot of plums.
The plums will be on sale.

They will be that week's loss leader.
We know how it will end—cars
aslant on the highway, grocery
store windows smashed and

empty, all of us empty. I will be
the one to bury them, one body
at a time I will bury them, one
hole at a time dug in the graveyards

and cemeteries, in the backyards
and empty fields. My shoulders will

grow strong, my hands will widen
and solidify. Every morning I will

wake up wondering if I am dead
yet; every night I will go to bed and
pray. When I close my eyes I will
create any room I want around me—

my childhood bedroom, the living
room of my best friend, the room where
a man first held me down. Funny—
I could take any of them, sleep in any

bed, but I will keep to my own.
Routine is good. All the bodies in
the ground, all the bodies rolled
and lowered. I will kiss each one

on the mouth. I will take each
hand and wash it and press it to
my cheek and let it go. I will think
about the things the fingers know

and will not know them. Every breast
and testicle, every skull and rib
will keep its secret. When it is done,
when everyone has lost their faith

around me, I will sit on the only
unturned earth and light a fire, and
burn the scraps that carry my name, but
I will not burn. I am already burning.

Why Not

Ruth Foley

Your ribcage is an octopus, inescapable.
My indexes are intercostal. The grasp

of your starfish fingers is chemical,
not physical. Your heart is thoroughly
chambered. I blend with the sea from

above, with the air from below. You
surface to regulate pressure. I rarely

surface, rarely regulate. I never count
the plummeting seconds. You calculate
your depths. You convince yourself

of science. The seagrass of your tendons
tells me otherwise. The heart feels unfair

because it's true. Sometimes I think
everything is chemotaxis. We might share
driftwood bones. Your ulna is a sea snake.

My radius an eel. Neither of us trusts
the availability of dissolved oxygen.

In Paradise

Trina Gaynon

Landscape gardeners put spot lights
on newly planted palm trees so they need
never stand in the dark.

Across the tract,
a tree removal firm
takes down a pair
of palm trees
grown so tall
no one dares
to climb the trunks
to cut away
dead fronds.
It takes a crane
and two men
to saw them down
from the crowns
to the sandy ground.
So the palms will never again
have to stand in the dark.

Sleep Study

Trina Gaynon

Without your weight as a counterbalance
in bed, I am at sea, floating, awake
to the music of a distant ocean.
The restless motion of the full-moon tide
moves in and out of my wintery dreams.

Tonight the stars will forget how to dance
and, though it rises, the full moon will ache
until you throw our front door open wide,
greet the beagle, and let in the sun's beams.

Tonight I picture you in the distance,
your arms and legs constantly in motion.
You snore, no one to roll you on your side.

After seven years, even asleep, we're a team.
I wait for your blessing: Deep sleep, sweet dreams.

That Day the Sky Was Stone

Gail Goepfert

Had the sky been stone or powder?
    Had it been February,
        I might have heard the *wheet*
    of the finches scouting seed.
Nothing but a *wheeze wheeze*
    from her oxygen machine.

My mother lay leaden—
    once in a while
        a muddled wakening, an urgent
    gesture with her hand, quelled
        by meds each time.
If only we'd known
    something was wrong—
the catheter
    blocked for days.

The nurse   who should have known
    came to make the change.
      Coiled   on the floor
        in the back of the house
knees   to   chest,
    fingers   jammed in my ears
        humming   in my throat
  to deaden my mother's cries,
        I knit my ire
      into my flesh.

Heartbeat
After Chagall's Bride under the Canopy

Hedy Habra

With eyes shut, he sees through me
will my bride's kiss be full of sweetness
can I be that woman he wishes for
sweetness sweeter than wine
they say passion is a carmine flower
I imagine her myrrh-scented hair
soon red petals will stain my bed
without having to say a word
I shiver as a transparent leaf
what if she feels my knees shaking
does he dream of a red-haired courtesan
we sat under the poplar's shade
my body was anointed with musk
the elders have gone to sleep
where did all the violins go
what if what lies behind her veil
I wish tomorrow were yesterday
we walked side by side in the olive grove
I am a wingless dove caught in his arms
I have scattered flowers under her steps
how can I hide my budding chest.

Once Upon a Time, an Olive Tree

Hedy Habra

My elders were chopped down and burned,
their roots too deep to uproot, rhizomes spread,

shoots spoke in tongues, mapping the field,
an invisible presence throbbing under the earth,

thirsting for each raindrop, remembering every bird's
trill and nest, the air redolent with blossoms,

the smell of grilled skewers, baking stones,
freshly roasted coffee, feet stomping the earth

with joy, a rhythm of life inscribed in every pore.
Will children ever know how much I miss their

lacy shadow woven with stories and wisdom?

Visiting my Mother in Montreal

Hedy Habra

Your slender legs,
        now withered stems, pores
exude the water your heart
        can no longer manage.
A nurse changes dressings daily, a blessing
your artist's eyes have dimmed so much,

I think of Balzac's
        excoriating ulcers and bedsores,
his stinking bed,
        your hands turning pages,
your portraits' delicate complexions.
My sister, the sole caretaker.

I'd come to visit,
        a falsetto weaving bright notes
into a weathered canvas
        with my silk nightgown,
my appetite, books, students' papers,
writing pads, all too colorful to bear,

I had to mold and fold,
        change key, fade within.

estate sale

Taylor Hamann

every word i spoke
to the dealer felt
like drinking bees

from a coffee mug.
they stung the scalloped
tissue of my throat

and all you would
offer was a line
of ink on the paper.

i did not want
her belongings,
but now, we have a barn

owl on the wall
that you say looks
just like your dead

ex-girlfriend.
it's the eyes, you say.
those are her eyes.

Devouring Silence
after Birch Trees, *artist Osnat Tzadok*

A.J. Huffman

Mist hovers, an echo of Birch bark, white
and gray amalgamation, filling the forest
with tangible breath. I imagine these sentinel
trunks as teeth. Poppies and leaves, reflections
of gums. Forest as mouth. The image speaks
to me in soothing voice of possibility. I close
my eyes, welcome its bite.

Exhumation
on the occasion of Pablo Neruda's exhumation, April, 2013

Lois P. Jones

After forty years in the dark, your bones
reenter the living in a morning light
that *slowly opens like a languid fruit.*

The surf still sings your praises at Isla Negra,
crashing amidst the chaos. What does it care
for those who surround your tomb

with their wheelbarrows and rumors
of poison? You have already moved past
the *shuddering walls in your struggle*

between matter and light. The loam lifts
from your grave as they carry your coffin
of air. They will send your body

to foreign lands and attempt to decipher
your fire. I grieve but not for you.
I grieve for all of us who spent the night

in your arms with our moon full
of candles. We will write the saddest lines.
Write, for example that truth is a star

over a foggy breakwater and death –
a black island with no boat to carry you home.

Self-Portrait As Ice Cream Truck

Allison Joseph

Always welcome, I glide through your
neighborhood, one repeating tune
on an endless loop to seduce
the smallest and eldest out
of barricaded homes and into

the streets, crying as if the
Messiah's come. Loyal to all
my flavors—you cannot—do not—
resist me, knowing all it takes
is a pocketful of change

to the man inside me to get
what I have to give: frozen
sugar on a stick, chocolate
frosted into submission,
sandwiches you nibble and lick

as if you'll never be granted
another, glorious soft-serve
squeezed into spirals and curls.
I am here to make you lose
your minds, make you forget

your diet and your last name,
every cell in your timid body
ready to shove a six-year-old
should she dare cut in front.
Cold as they come, I got you

on lock, silver body stealthy
on these ordinary streets, sleek

machine full of rainbows and push-ups,
strawberry shortcake and bomb-poms.
Should you try to resist me,

if you stay silent while everyone
clamors for my sweet tastes,
I'll make sure my music
never leaves your brain,
endless loop stunning you.

To Know a Poet

Allison Joseph

is to know a lunatic,
raver in regular clothing,
class clown too broken

for makeup, bruiser
with flailing fists,
trying to make contact

with skin you never touch.
How strange we must seem—
full of stuttering songs

and shy revelations,
muttering about syllables
and shade, tipsy

with rhythms that pulse
behind every third eye.
How frustrating it is

to speak with us—
constant leaks of languid
metaphor, bundles of similes

tangled as telephone wire.
I could tell you
to befriend us,

feed us through
our multiple hungers,
clothe us during slippery

phases of nightblind
madness. But I warn you,
what we have is

contagious—
a mutant strain
always evolving,

seeping in
through your eyes
to occupy your brain,
make your nights
with unendurable ache,
that ever-decreasing faith.

Dew Etc.

Alan S. Kleiman

I feel wet
not rain like but dew
like du, du liegst mir im Herzen do
like call me in the night do
like remember me in the darkness of the day do
like don't leave any stone turned up do
like don't without me do.

Temptation, Passed

Laurie Kolp

Suctioned,
a loathsome slimy snail
on paneled wall

its trail of mucus
met with vacant eyes
close enough to recognize
runway tracks.

Nicotine lingers
in crevices
like my late mother
chanting, *don't do it.*

How many times
she said, *don't do it,*
and yet she did. *Do it.*

I offer up
a hasty prayer
asking God
not to let me do it.

Layer upon layer,
the shell I tried for years
to strip away and failed.

Erosion spirals back
to barren core
every single time.

I turn toward the snail
and breathe.
It hasn't moved much,
but it's moved.

Stonehenge

Richard Krawiec

You expect the deflated football, the empty bottle of Gatorade, by the creek half a mile from the cul de sac. But the bed of moss anchored by two dun mushrooms, tops upturned like tulips, makes you look again, past the eroded bank, across the streambed of rocks and sand, over the bell tone tickle of the creek to the small Stonehenge circle of sticks and bark, alignment of worship built by some small god, hands too tiny to make an altar of his life.

In the distance commuters grumble cars back home to their prayers of craft beers and dancing with the human stars. While the small god lays on his bed dreaming of moss and sunsets and the way light might align through wooden arches to pierce his life, bolt him alive.

We are the small gods of our island of moss, our bodies arched, formed from neither sarsen or bluestone, bark or stick. I balance above, knees and hands to the sweet cool. Your hair curls sungold on the green, glints and shines even in the day's decline, a bright jagged, light that pierces a passageway through our precarious balance, embrace that glows, a burn that will seal it open.

Aphrodite and the Gods of Love

Rustin Larson

The writer thinks about Aphrodite and the Gods
Of Love. Although the writer is an occupant
Of the large dark house I often find myself
In when I dream, I don't know the writer by name,
Nor have I seen his face. I've seen his shadows.
Why is he thinking about this? Perhaps it's all
He ever thinks of. What color hair does
Aphrodite have? Is she night or is she fair?
When you call her name is anyone there?

I think of the islands I've stepped upon,
Maybe even slept upon. Manhattan is an island.
There are islands in the Mississippi River.
I believed I sailed past an island in the Bay
Of Fundy. England is upon an island,
Though I've never been there. There are
Islands created by snow melt on sidewalks.
I've found spilled drinks on café tables
Can create temporary islands of dry surface.
Then floods creep in and dampen
The napkins. No single person is an island,
Although I would argue both for and against that.
A guitar standing in a corner is an island full
Of sleeping sounds. Memory is an island
To which we retreat.
The car racing down the boulevard
Has the throaty sound of T-Rex in its tail pipe.
This little town is an island; it is a distant
Planet from which no one returns.

Dreams

Rustin Larson

I think of dreams I've had: the shrinking
Room; the rooftop dream where Hitler
Is on his rooftop, and I am on mine;
A soldier cried scanning the sky for zeppelins;
They never came; the dream where
We travel by train and the distant cities
Crumble; it is frightening; there is the dream
Where I cover canvases with dripping black
Wax; the dream of boxes of coins, or hillsides
Of coins unearthed; the guitar that makes
No sound; the endless fountain; I am
The fountain; the sky in which questions
Want to become people; the grassy fields
Where birds walk on shadows that form
A Ouija board; the dream of the cafeteria
That always runs out of food; the brick
Walls that open upon rooms furnished
With the ugly oranges and greens and
Owls of my childhood; the pregnant woman
With the skeleton's head; the dream
Where I stand in an auditorium where I take
Forever to introduce a poem; when I recite
The poem, I stand silent with my eyes closed.
Everyone closes their eyes. The reading
Is canceled. It will never happened again;
And there's the dream of the girl I kissed
In college. She died when she was 55.
I dream that I am sitting at a table with her.
I have a pile of Halloween chocolate bars
In front of me. She asks, "May I have one?"
I say, "Take all or part or several of any."
She looks at me like I'm insane. "Why

Would I just want part of one?" she says,
And then rakes in the whole pile like winnings
At a roulette table. "You know," I say,
"you don't look a day older than..." and then
I realize where she's been, and then I wake.

Homecoming

Sean Lause

There are many voices.
They come like bees
to hive your heart
and sting dark memories to light.

And light to light
is poetry of angels,
their blood at dawn
spreading wonder to the real.

Trust your veins to sing
like wind through a spider web
that clutches the sun
in an ecstasy of hunger.

Feel your nerve ends turn luminous
like snake eyes in the moon.
Let touch turn your love electric,
both warmth and power.

There is a tree whose leaves are meanings
only you may set free.
Begin where a streetlamp regards eternity.
Follow a bridge where breaths draw near.

Now your flesh is no longer mystery,
nor a crime to be cruelly solved,
but a hymn of its own homecoming
to the earth for which it longed.

What are your hands but shattered flames
meant to caress the stars? Open your heart
to the suffering of stones, the swan questioning
silence, the word dreaming of the rose.

Hospitalized in December

Helen Losse

I look back—
through silvery linen-shades
on east-facing windows—
at Winston-Salem,
black, dotted with fireflies,

especially through the shade left
one-quarter open in my ninth-floor
room. As the city wakes, I realize bugs
are actually street lights, and when

I squint, Matchbox cars creep along I-40.
A siren screams; a truck horn sounds.
The horizon flames: rose-red in color
changes to rust. Navy blue clouds

navigate a brightening sky, smoke
curls upward. The charge nurse
enters, breaking my chain of thought.
I am accustomed by this time—

from the experience of previous days—
to the sting of a needle-prick.
And with this particular nurse—
who draws blood on the count of three—

the procedure hurts. It was also she
who inserted my NG tube. A friend, who
had one inserted, called it "waterboarding."
Pushing my hands under a blanket to

combat my urge to smack, that nurse
crammed the tube down, so my body
would give information. "Drink," she said.
Today I am able to manage a smile.

Today I go home, where I'll miss only
the Moravian star. Hauled, on a clear day
in late November, to the twelfth-floor
rooftop, its 27 points shed multiple

lumens of light. Every December
the star helps God and the never-sleeping
hospital keep watch. I walk to the window
to see it. But tonight, at home,

surrounded by hallmarks of season:
packages of warmth, stockings of joy,
candles, a tree of love, I'll only
remember the star.

Medicine Circle

Ken Meisel

All night the stars in the sky exploded like rattles,
    and they fell to the earth

like granite fragments into the medicine circle
    that I'd chosen for myself,

and once, struck by one of those bright stones,
    I no longer felt so afraid of the frigid icing

of the stars and the floating moon
    swirling above me in electrified loneliness.

A small frog jumped into my circle.
    I watched it long-jump a pile of oak leaves

and it landed right next to my quivering hand
    as I held a flashlight to it,

and then it hopped into my open palm
    and I felt it mark me – quickly –

across the long vein there like an inoculation
    against something I'd always dreaded,

which then became the clan I would belong to –
    amphibious, croaking, poetic.

And I knew the shape of my solid bones
    into liquids, and the red blood

coursing through my wrist
    became a wiggling snake as I lifted

a dewy rock to hold it high
        to the moon ascending wide awake –

and suddenly I entered the galaxy in a canoe
        and I rowed the universe alone.

And the night insects rose and fell
        around me

in an electric, translucent bourree,
        in a kind of silent delirium

until I became quenched of all the thirst
        that my intellectual reason

had choked to dry dirt inside of me.
        And sometime, during the final act

of my night-rowing dream, I was baptized
        in a raging thunder storm –

which then became my new medicine name
        against all the other names

that had misidentified me for years upon years
        as just this man of preoccupation and skin.

On the west coast of Michigan, in Petoskey,
        my father – after fishing –

collapsed into the silent, foam-filled truncation
      of a heart attack, and he

slowly slipped through an opened portal
      like a silenced guitar,

his skeleton, like a Les Paul guitar box
      shattered asunder,

the silver strings of his rib cage
      snapping open to release his soul.

At four am I heard the urgent calls of a shriek owl
      piercing my dream in the pines.

At dawn, the sun melted
      through the opaque distillery

of clouds spreading open
      into ruffled curtains beyond

the horizon, and a grown man strolled
      through swamp sumac –

as if he were a mysterious messenger,
      blessing me home.

Watching Bilal Fall

Ken Meisel

Because in the Arabic, the name Bilal, or Billy,
    when spoken in its native
        Middle Eastern tongue,

means, "The Chosen One,"
    we watch Bilal fall.
        He *is* falling –

like a zodiac of chosen twilight
    from a dilapidated window
        high up in The Brewster Projects.

He has been rousted
    from his reverie –
        during his deep contemplation

of the city nudging her silver face
    through a wedding veil of clouds for him to kiss,
        by four who wish to rob him –

right here, beneath the starlight as he skateboards
    across an abandoned basketball court
        bathed in sunset,

and he's been shot in the face
    with a pistol and then laid out flat
        in a bed of weeds and debris,

even though he can barely
    speak English,
        and even though the money

he's carrying in his wallet will later be spent
   on fast food and weed.
      And even as he is expiring,

he knows that all who vanish must at first
   rise up –
      like a flame climbing up

a twisted tree branch –
   and so he rises up
      to the highest tower

of these vacant Brewster Projects,
   to fall.
      And so we watch

his elongated, slender body
   spiraling downward,
      into wood piles and bindweed.

He is aiming himself down like a squid,
   into the ribboned twist and swirl
      of chaos.

Isn't this what the artist studies –
   the unpredictable twist
      and swirl of chaos?

Isn't this what we volunteer to marry –
   alchemists in artistry –
      even at the time of dying?

And so he falls like a squid
>   freeing himself
>   from the familiar

aurora of nerves and lather –
>   from the lock-up of his bone structure –
>   like he is still within the instant,

even now, because the wonder
>   of this experience
>   is too aerial for him to miss.

And like all who have been chosen
>   to resemble a star
>   unveiling its five-pointedness

from birth robe to jaw bone
>   to white glissando matter,
>   we watch him demonstrate

his falling – through the air like a super nova –
>   into this cradle of plank wood,
>   lying there like his coffin.

It's not the city's fault, you say –
>   she was only the new bride in his eyes
>   because he'd blessed her that way.

It's not the killers' fault, nor the projects,
>   for they were simply there
>   to teach the meaning of how we are chosen.

And because he is the chosen one
        we watch him
                open his giant squid eyes

like a deep water diver
        as he drives his gaze
                into the grid arteries of the savage city.

And he spins and he needles in –
        freeing himself of all matter,
                into his next graffiti splatter.

And from his mouth come the words,
        "I'm savagely wild. *I am...*"
                This is how I am chosen.

Monsters from the Id

Corey Mesler

*"For the moment, / with the moment,
she is young and in love."*
—Heather Minette

There is want and
there is a third thing.
The woman and the
man are made of
wax. They mold each
other because they
grasp that's what
men and women do.
He takes his hands
and expunges the stretch
marks across her
downy middle. She
grips the center of him,
a mandrake root,
as if it could hold it-
self. For a moment
it sways them both.
This is all in an-
other place, a place of
fantasy, dereliction and
peace. There *is* such
a place where desire is
more than the second thing.

My body asks

Corey Mesler

My body asks
but does not
like the answers.
I move from
base to worse.
The heat is up
and I am breath-
ing. You were
here a tick ago,
a glint, may-
be a spark. I know
better than
to ask more
than my body does.

Lines from Base Camp

Naila Moreira

The silence reminds
that aloneness is all there is—
that on the edge of a great crag
we stand waiting,
a cliff behind us
and a chasm before us,
wide space beside us
and black night above us,
and that within the self,
as dark as the great depths,
it is there we create the beloved

Cleave

M. Nasorri Pavone

Therefore shall a man leave his father and mother, and shall cleave unto his wife: and they shall be one flesh.
[Genesis 2:24] Bible.

While it means to split, to divide,
it also means to adhere, to cling.

A word that travels back and forth
in either direction like a subway train.

His face took on a wide-eyed expression
after his wife died. They'd been severed

at their most inseparability. Bonded.
Broken. Bonded. If one word were to signify

both birth and death it wouldn't be
confusing, for they work as bookends:

a butter knife with a serrated edge,
the hammer with its claw,

the pencil mated to the worn eraser tip.
With one toggle switch, we go on and off.

Girl Flying A Kite

Jonathan K. Rice

She tosses her kite into the wind that skips
off crests of waves unfurling upon the shore.

Her arms outstretched toward the sea,
she dances upon the wet sand.

Gulls cry, flutter about. The kite, a silent bird,
becomes a distant orange speck.

In one final ascent the string frees itself
and the kite is gone.

Desire

Judith Skillman

Long after a woman
accepts the rack of age,
intolerant overseer
with his bloodied instruments,

a vestige of passion clings.
Like the appetite of boiled milk
for its skin, or a winter day
for the sun. Like the single

marigold blooming
on a veranda—
that stubborn, red-headed child.
Long into the lateness of life,

after the shadow puppets
of parents have been pulled
from the theatre,
their heads twisted off—

deep inside the body
an extravagant wish surfaces,
requests to play the part
of descant.

Queen Anne's Lace

Judith Skillman

No longer noxious,
not hogweed, merely
the poorest, most flagrant
example of a wild flower
exhaling musk.
If you vest yourself
in dreams
do you sleep?
If, in the poor times,
you remember
other ornaments,
embellished Persian carpets
and crystal,
does memory render
you rich? Put finger
and thumb
to the stem, green
with endless oils
and honey, milk
drips siphoned
into the throat
to take away
the scrim of sweat.
Pull this weed
from the earth.
You deserve to pluck
one free dessert
after all the coveting
you've done.
When they ask
why it sits
on the counter

in a simple water bottle,
smile with your broken
teeth, grin
the fear of the judged.
Expect heaven
will be no more
than a scrap
of impoverished cloud,
a wisp improbable
as this moment
of subtracting
one more token
from a place
in which you worked
to become only,
finally, common.

This Shade So Early Clings
After Le Peignoir Bleu, *by Henri Lebasque, 1920*

Joannie Stangeland

Night rinsed pale as watercolor stars
lifts above your shoulders, vanishes

beyond that lilac mountain, your morning framed
by sheer curtains, the balcony's iron ornament,

but past the window, the trees' green and a sky
that washes softer than blue, nearly clear
to inspire, inhale, one cloud enough

to make you see a lucky rabbit,
a duck the dawn pearls and leaves.

You strike a bargain, feel the sun
stroke your throat as the world opens

like a shell, or the peephole in the egg you saw as a girl,
glimpse of a meadow in miniature,

memory breathing still beneath your ribs,
the dream that hovers, dust in the light.

Below, the cat snakes ankles
for cream or an old fish head.
Birds begin their arias again.

When you hear a child sing, you'll slip
this cobalt robe and quiet, join the hours on the ground,
the day's aches and taxes.

Chiding the Muse

Annie Stenzel

Make it new. — Ezra Pound

The fact is, all those fresh and fancy ways of saying things
are gone, and we're obliged to sit like tailors
with our scissors and our shipboard needle
trying to make or mend an impossible garment.
Make it how? With these pickled tools, husks of hands
and stomped-on shards of old significance?

It's as though you hire an architect for your dandy
custom structure, but then the builder
tries to frame the place with 2 x 4s warped
from the desert sun, or torqued by standing
water, the wood so compromised the grain now spurns
the saw, forbids the very entrance of a nail.

But since I'm still dumbfounded by the capsized
starbowl of an winter night; still court the sweet
pain caused by drawing breath when lilac is in bloom—
how tragic that the very threat of speech forfeits these miracles.
You told us, make it new, and don't I wish I could
depict the merest fraction of the indescribable.

Yet how, when Babel's weight has crushed
the juice from every single syllable?
How, when the word "rose" no more evokes that
sense-rejoicing synthesis of petals and fragrance
than the word "I" denotes this woman who struggles
with a suitcase of self stuck in an envelope of skin.

Dreams & Dismemberment

After Magritte

Maria Terrone

The eyes of the chalk-faced
   man in the bowler hat
      are   closed.   Maybe
we see his death
         mask,   maybe
he ponders "The Meaning of Night,"
         the painting
he finds himself
   boxed   inside.

His double, or himself
   reversed, turns
to the sea, head and black coat
         a void.
An eyeless bird-woman
   planted in sand
strokes his back with one wing:
Leda and her rapist
         merged.

She is beaked now,
   hugging a human's gauntlet
to her feathered body,
      seam-hosed thighs cut
   by the frame.

The sky has shed scraps
   of cloud. They litter
the shore of this darkening
     sea that seeps
and spreads like ink through pores.

Provisions

Donna Vorreyer

Alone and out of ammunition,
I long for a pistol to punctuate
the silence, to send flash blasts
of em dash into the surreal dark.
For now, my sad revisions are
just crushed spheres of dirt
I hurl into the murder sounds
around me. This does not satiate
my fear. Before we separated,
we buried a stash of weapons,
made a home for them deep
in this meadow, a faint trickle
of birdsong easing our labor.
But that was before. Now there
is only a charred field of holes.
I charge the valley like a horse
ridden rough– wild, ragged,
and praying for death.

When a Person Carries Darkness Inside

Martin Willitts Jr.

When people carry darkness inside,
it does not bode well for anyone.
When they are cramped-up like a fist,
brief violence leaving its marks,
then step aside. Nearness is like being
blindfolded while reviving a chainsaw.

There was a man who wore strangeness:
face-stained, one eye stroke-stretched
like uncooked egg yolk or sediment
at the edge of a moving river. Adults said
this is what happens to sinners.

My father said some dogs are beaten
until their tail goes limp, flinching from touch.
Mother suggested some people are darkness
infested by wasps, because they were abused.

One day, I smiled at the man who wore strangeness;
he handed me an apple.

Some would have warned it could be poisoned
or stuffed with tiny pins.
But it was the best apple, ever.

Housewarming the Last House on Holland Island, Fallen into the Bay

Sarah Ann Winn

I pull on neoprene, check
to make sure the seals are tight. Take time.
I have to dwell for a moment on
pressure. Our old house, stranded there
under the waves, perhaps has
already found the deepest
chasm to teeter over.
Minutes swim like little blind
fish in and out of windows.
Current flutters the curtains.
Stay begs the house, and the light
unravels in wavering
skeins above. A reminder.

Even with the mask, my mouth
feels silted, krilled. To measure
time, I mark my way across
the sand on the kitchen floor,
pace a pattern, a zen garden,
where you are the fifteenth
stone, always hidden.
I tend the things you left -
the birch basket curling, long
ago waterlogged, the hair
band under the fridge.
A bivalve falls in love with
your old butterfly hair clip.
On the desk, a sea fan cools
the obsidian paperweight.

I stare out the window
at the Titanic in the distance,
imagine the shape of a cloud
on the blue wall of a passing blue whale.
Plan to forget, to throw everything out
in a slow shatter glass cloud of loss
and sand. Settled, it will give
over to coral in time.
Memory's not waterproof,
not forever, not for long.

Taste the Wind

Nancy Wilson

The leaves fall, for me, for you,
if you want it
close your eyes and feel the breeze
it blows for me, for you,
if you want to

The colors of the leaves tell me
that life is short, feel me now,
before I leave
I'll be here for awhile,
to taste the wind.

Wednesday
(Asia Pacific Museum, Pasadena, CA)

Nancy Wilson

Golden specks of light falling,
(sparkles) (lites)
from branches above,
thoughts pondering along the way,
pictures of poets and apples,
the leaves take on the sun
I wish I could capture

Every morning blue,
water flows, with a peace
stars are clear, and above
maybe a distant planet.

Maurice Utrillo: Portraitist of Street and Sky

Bill Yarrow

He's drunk again, a king beneath his throne
but what does she know, Susanne Valadon?

At him always, pestering him with unanswerable questions, why does he paint this, why doesn't he paint that, he doesn't know, he just paints, things that strike him, the things he sees, a dim shadow on a monument, twisted sunlight on an awning, the blue hieroglyphics of decay, a cat in the wine, the white endless façade of homes, the pink and grey of skies in love with loneliness. She watches as he stirs. Oblivious of everything, he rises, washes out his eyes, pours water through a spoon of sugar into his glass and begins to sip his pale-green drink. Absinthe makes the heart grow fonder. His canvas parts its lips and puckers. He grabs his Muse by the waist and pulls her toward him, presses his middle against her middle, his chest against her breasts, digs his fingers into her curls, pulls at the elastic of her blouse, her shoulders, suddenly, shockingly bare, her lower throat open to his open mouth, she's all a mess, dishabille, in disarray, his hurried fingers take up the brush, a splash of paint, a daub of color, sips of silver, hatch of black, a wipe of white, lush squares of pastel tints, the second-story windows begin to form, enfeebled trees sprout up, the horizon is firmly planted around the corner, behind the alley, just beneath the burgeoning sky. What does this mean? *What does what mean?* Where are the people? *They have not yet been born.* Overhead, mawkish gulls begin to weep daylight into the marsh. The gutters blush as men in bloody aprons take their business to their walls. Priests in red robes bend their tonsures toward eternity, or so it seems to him, supine, head wedged against the bookcase, mouth agape, dreaming of dangers, his feet perpendicular to the floor.

His mother shakes her greying head and sighs.
The paint along the bottom edge is dry.

Poe Pound Villanelle

Bill Yarrow

The sands of time are changed to golden grains
the coaches are perfumed wood
while only thine eyes remain.

A thought arose within the human brain:
not all our power is gone, not all our fame.
The sands of time are changed to golden grains.

Be eager to find new evils and new good.
I will get me to the wood
for only thine eyes remain.

Ruffle the skirts of prudes!
Halo of hell and with a pain
the sands of time are changed to golden grains.

Bowed from wild pride into shame
by heaven, his horses are tired
but only thine eyes remain.

Dancing in transparent brocade
let us therefore cease from pitying the dead
The sands of time are changed to golden grains
and only thine eyes remain.

Spontaneous Tranquility

Bill Yarrow

The sea will never show the stamp of who she was
for, inured to moonlight, honor craves no human bones.
Once upon a time, I held a palpable ghost, impervious
to lace, but her pulse, it was, forgivably, quotidian.

No roughness will she inhere, no fission inhabit;
she is deaf to dumb implacability. O, who has made
her sleep so deep? She is inevitably dispersed, existing
only as song, rising sharply out of magma and wave.

When We Marry: A Poem in Two Voices

Bill Yarrow

when we marry, the river
and the wind will kiss, the
sun and the sea will dance, the
moon and the trees will sing

    when we marry, the cornice
    will embrace the nave, the
    transom will buff the lintel,
    the gable will embark on
    the eaves

when we marry, the wind
and the trees will dance, the
river and the sea will sing, the
sun and the moon will kiss

    when we marry, the clavier
    will excise the choir, the
    overture will traduce the
    etude, the galliard will eclipse
    the hymn

when we marry, the wind
and the moon will sing, the
sea and the sun will kiss, the
river and the trees will dance

    when we marry, the fallacies
    will recede, the firmament will
    rescind, the folderol
    will relent

Showcases

Lois P. Jones
and
Allison Joseph

Lois P. Jones
Poet, Photographer, and Radio Host Incomparable

by Elizabeth Nichols

Photo: George Jisho Robertson

Amidst the sonance of contemporary poets, Lois P. Jones and her body of work resonate sui generis.

Jones is a poet consciously attuned to the call of her muse, and one wholly immersed in the creative life. Sound and thought are fluid in Jones' work, exploring with ease the liminality of the conscious and unconscious. A strong spiritual core is at the center of Jones' poetry, which is simultaneously personal and universal. Her poems are spontaneous and flexible and of astonishing beauty, tenderness, and strength. In her poems, the reader will find juxtapositions of harmony and dissonance—life in all its complexity.

Jones' poetry has appeared in numerous publications, including *Pirene's Fountain*, *Narrative Magazine*, *Tupelo Quarterly*, and *American Poetry Journal* as well as several acclaimed poetry anthologies. In addition, Jones' work won honors under judges Kwame Dawes, Fiona Sampson,

Ruth Ellen Kocher, and others. She is the winner of the 2012 *Tiferet* Poetry Prize and is a multiple Pushcart nominee.

Originally from Chicago, Jones currently resides in California where she hosts the Los Angeles radio show, *Poets Cafe*, and co-produces the Moonday Poetry Reading Series. In addition to her many roles, Jones is also the poetry editor for the *Kyoto Journal* and an interviewer at *American Microreviews and Interviews*. Jones acted as a moderator for two online poetry forums for five years and participated in competitions on those forums, such as the long-running Web de Sol contest. In fact, Jones' poems have won first, second, or third place in those competitions eight times since 2008. In 2010, Jones' poem "Ouija" received the Poem of the Year award from New Yorker staff writer Dana Goodyear in 2010. Jones attended the San Miguel Poetry Week from 2005-2010 as a workshop participant with some of the most distinguished poets writing in English today, including Willis Barnstone, Mark Doty, Glyn Maxwell, and Paul Muldoon. Jones is also a passionate photographer, and a number of her photographs are professionally published. On her photography, Jones says, "The same principles which apply to good poetry, also apply to the photographic image—a sense of composition, aspects of shadow and light, a lyric quality, a narrative arc no matter how small as well as an established sense of mystery." In this showcase feature, Jones' striking photos are placed beside her equally emotive poetry.

Jones' poetic vision is reminiscent of Rainer Maria Rilke's grave, mysterious, and beautiful work. As in Rilke's *Duino Elegies*, Jones' clear articulation and fluent ideas bring out a luminous quality in her work. In her poetry, there is lyrical intensity and permeability. What makes Jones' work special is her ability to penetrate—like light breaking the dark—into what is meaningful and important to each reader.

Jones' poetry transports the reader. The inner life of the speaker—of the human—is pried "wide open as the window," and the reader is invited to "come in." Her poetry tells a narrative through rich imagery and language that taps into all the senses. Whether the reader listens to mariachis in San Miguel or travels to "Calle Canal," there is always a deeper connection at hand, allowing the reader to viscerally experience place through poetry and thereby plumb the emotional landscape of the human heart. In "The Scent of Ariel," published in *Tiferet* and for which she won the 2012 *Tiferet* Poetry Prize, Jones' speaker describes the pleasure taken in transience—of seeking the self in the other. *Pirene's Fountain* editors were privileged to hear Jones read "The Scent of Ariel" in person at Glass Lyre Press' Live Lyre reading event this year.

The Scent of Ariel

When the shuttle arrives at the old wooden door,
luggage bulging with too many shoes
and *gringa* lotions, books she won't have time to open,
when the teenage boy smiles after hauling the world

four flights of terra cotta steps to her room
with views of Calle Canal and the red rooftops
clinging to early winter warmth, it won't be
the earthy scent of pink geraniums outside her window

or last night's wood smoke and kerosene
that fills her lungs, but the freshly washed shirt
of the boy, neat as his perfect teeth, the scent –
part lather, part lavender. She won't call it innocence,

though it comes close. Closer is the lack of artifice,
the way she tries to lose her skin by slipping
into cotton, the comfort of towels laundered
in sunshine. And if this country is not hers,

if some resent her pale flesh, still Ariana
remembers her each year and brings extra towels
that smell sweet as a first kiss, rough as a night
of too many sangrias when bells

of the Parroquia jangle like cast iron pans,
and she believes every tourist is a burro
without a master, grazing on what it can,
pretending there is somewhere to belong.

There is a tangible vitality in Jones' poetry. Even when Jones' work contemplates death, energy flows in the stanzas, each word an affirmation—a pulse beating a tattoo on the psyche. In "Unmarked Grave," the speaker elegizes the death of poet Federico Garcia Lorca. A beautiful dissonance exists in this poem as images of "rotten oranges," "white sheets," and a "sensual tongue" create an unavoidable din of life that clashes against the final reality of death. With the scent of "basil" lingering, the reader understands that death can underscore life and, in doing so, celebrates the departed.

Unmarked Grave

*All I want is a single hand,
A wounded hand if that is possible.*
— Federico Garcia Lorca

Beautiful man, with your brows of broken ashes
and eyes that migrate in winter,

a hollow in your hand
where the moon fell through.

I could have kissed your mouth,
passed an olive with my tongue,
the aftertaste of canaries on our breath.

But the shriek of the little hour
is spent, and there is no road back.

The day it happened
there were no good boys
or dovecots filled with virgins,

just a sun imploding
like a sack of rotten oranges,

the scent of basil
from the grove near your home
and the piano that still waits for you.

No one will remember
the coward who shot you,
but the sheets,

the white sheets you sail on,
coming home.

Published in *American Poetry Journal*

At the heart of Jones' poetry, the reader can find a reverence for existence. Her work is a simultaneous celebration of the beauty of life and language, and the power of poetry. In "Birthday," the speaker is "aflame in wonder, / unconcerned with what occupies the dark." In "Locals Listen to the Mariachi Band at El Jardin in San Miguel," the smell of beer and churros summons visions of "*family*" and "*language*."

And, in "How She Paints Herself," the body becomes an effervescent vessel: a symbol of a life reverently, and fully, lived. In Jones' poetry, life is painted in strokes of simile, metaphor, and awe.

How She Paints Herself
   after Susan Dobay's "Awakening"

Sometimes the yearning
burns so fiercely
it illumines a body

worthy of Gnostic devotion.
Better to paint one's self
from the inside out

better to believe in the light
that limns the brush.
Faith is in your hand —

in the way you reveal yourself
as an autumnal river,
dark moss jewelling

your inner thighs, flesh
fully exposed, sprawled
so comfortably below

the surface of things. Sunlight
kindles your waist,
defines your belly

as a golden island, a future
without need of horizon.
And your smile, satisfied

the way a woman knows
how to please herself
You lie back, elbows up,

welcoming the world
as lover. You were never
really a virgin,

Every part of you
meant to be known
born to say yes.

Published in *Awakenings*.

    Jones' work makes the reader revel in life, shaken but exhilarated. She has the rare ability to open the reader to his vulnerabilities and desires. It is no wonder that Lois P. Jones is a poet so admired and loved, and one whose work has received awards and the attention of major voices in the poetry field. There is subtlety and restraint in her work, but also a welcome accessibility. Her unique diction and quicksilver imagery are woven by some strange alchemy into poetry that transforms and transcends, trembling with inner light.

Pirene's Fountain thanks Lois P. Jones for the interstitial photographs in this feature.

In Conversation with Poet and Radio Host Lois P. Jones

Interviewed by Elizabeth Nichols

Welcome to Pirene's Fountain, Lois! As the submissions editor, I have had the pleasure of reading your work, and I can attest firsthand that not only is it crafted beautifully, it is also deeply resonant with layered meaning and emotion. Please tell us the story of Lois P. Jones, the poet. How did your early experiences crystallize into writing poetry?

Thank you for your kind words, Elizabeth. I am grateful to the Pirene's Fountain team for inviting me to share my work and process. I came rather late to poetry. My first love was sketching and up to my 12th year I was primarily interested in portraiture. I dabbled in poetry in my early teens as most of us do but it wasn't until I spent time in Geneva, Switzerland that I had my first "awakening." Tucked quietly into a narrow street was a fabulous French restaurant, L'Opera Bouffe, where we enjoyed a specially prepared Valentine's Day dinner. The proprietress loved poetry, so she chose two poems to be placed at each place setting. The first was by Paul Verlaine and then another by Paul Eluard. It was Eluard whose surreal love poem came to me like an epiphany.

Premièrement

Mon amour pour avoir figuré mes désirs
Mis tes lèvres au ciel de tes mots comme un astre
Tes baisers dans la nuit vivante
Et le sillage de tes bras autour de moi
Comme une flamme en signe de conquête
Mes rêves sont au monde
Clairs et perpétuels.

Et quand tu n'es pas là
Je rêve que je dors je rêve que je rêve.

And when you are away
    I dream that I sleep, I dream that I dream.

Not a dream, but a point of awakening into a living dream. I fell into a world that felt like home. I continued to read the works of Eluard and other surrealists of the time. It wasn't until 2003 when I came across an ecstatic poem by Russell Salamon that I was moved to respond. It began an intense period of immersion, mentorship, and experimentation. I remember the pleasure of sitting on the floor of the Skylight Bookstore in Los Angeles and pulling random books that seemed to draw me in. I discovered the metaphysical poets who would be my gurus to this day—Rainer Maria Rilke, Federico Garcia Lorca, Jorge Luis Borges, Pablo Neruda, and others.

I attended workshops at San Miguel Poetry Week for five years as well as other workshops, including time in France with Pascale Petit. The four years on two excellent on-line poetry forums moderating, critiquing, and learning the art of revision enabled me to offer intensive feedback to my peers. I have a special affinity for Spanish language poets because of their ability to excite the imagination. Borges experimented with fiction and magical realism. He combined myth and the philosophical thought. Lorca's surreal leaps were and still are a great influence on my work. For me, reading poetry in translation is vital to gain a broader sense of the multitude of voices. So many—German, Polish, Russian, Chinese, Arabic, Persian—there is no language which excludes poetry. If we read only English language poets, it's like making the same soup every day. It may taste good but we limit our perceptions. I believe we are a part of every culture, every corner of the globe. The Irish poet, Seán Ó Ríordáin says, *there is nowhere in this world / That we were not born into.*

Could you talk a little bit about your writing process, and what makes a poem special for you? Tell us about some of the current projects that you are working on.

I think most imaginative people are intuitively tuned in to the world. I receive a number of creative urges throughout the day, most of which I don't act on because I don't have the time and attention to draw them out. This is why I'll often sign up for workshops on line. Having access to a particular course structure and theme helps to lure out dormant poems. In a perfect world I'd have plenty of time to retreat and read literature to help me focus on specific projects. We take what we can and balance the rest. I'm just past the ten-year point since I began writing and I feel I am still searching for my own voice. Some poets begin fully loaded while others take a lifetime, if ever, to achieve a genuine expression. The important thing is to continue to work toward one's authentic voice. It's good to have influences. Reading the work of others can't help but shape us. We take these voices in and they become a part of us until they constellate.

My best work often comes when traveling because I'm without routine distractions. While I sometimes write about the immediate experience, I often discover earlier travels resurface. I love being in the mode of transience when every sense is heightened.

What makes a poem special is a wonderful and challenging question to answer. Without sounding pretentious, and yet trying to find a way to express how a poem "opens" me would be to rely on another artist who achieves this distinction in film – Andrei Tarkovsky. Tarkovsky was known as the Russian poet of cinema. He had the creative capacity to draw in the metaphysical through the use of color to set apart different worlds, often presenting dreamlike images to tether symbolism, spirituality and philosophy into one arresting theme. In the way Tarkovsky uses light to create fourth dimensions (see the Andre Rublv bell casting scene), his facility with character, physicality and motion, so will a great poem use tone, caesura, space, sound, rhythm, strong nouns, powerful and surprising verbs, masterful simile and/or metaphor, certain universal archetypes (which allow us to personally penetrate the poem's interior and it, us) to draw us into The Zone, that world which is part reality and party myth with just the right amount of mystery. I want a great poem to take me into a world that is both foreign and familiar. It leads the reader by the bridle and by the end of the poem you are stunned by its brilliance. As my friend Peter Ludwin mentioned recently; "A poet with that kind of power is one you want to build a cabin for in your mind." Of course I love many other kinds of poetry! Poems of humor, of social conscious, philosophical, bold, wise, clever, silly – the entire poetic oeuvre. It is always a question of quality. A great poet achieves authenticity and never takes the reader out of the poem's "session." Perhaps poems which survive time are those which take on a richness in multiple readings. A great haiku, while it places you in the moment, may also be interpreted different ways or in a singular way which is absolutely original and profound.

While I am working on finishing my current manuscript I am very excited about my next project, which involves translation of a small work by an acquaintance of Rilke. I can't say too much about it. Right now it seems to hold potential. I am hoping to travel to Switzerland and do a residency or else a cheap Airbnb next year. Just in the dream stages now.

We would love to take a peek at your bookshelf! What writers have had a lasting impact on your work? What are you reading now?

Most of my books are in search of shelves. They are lying about in woven baskets, piled on my cedar chest and Chinese trunk, and wherever I can find an open space! I have a small place and only one and a half bookshelves and Rilke occupies two shelves in the tall case in my bedroom plus another portion of a shelf in my living room. There is no time, whether I am deeply inspired or heading through a dry patch that Rilke doesn't not speak to me through his correspondence, poetry and prose. I collect first editions and dream of owning a signed copy of anything. I've just checked Christies and a single page from 'Die spanische Trilogie' written in 1920 sells for $31,000! I'll have to save up for that... Some others in the "permanent" bookcase include Neruda, Lorca, Bobrowski, Borges, Machado, Pessoa, Hesse, Arseny Tarkovsky, Plath and Whitman. Some contemporaries include Galway Kinnel, Mary Oliver, Joseph Stroud, Peter Ludwin, Mark Doty, Joseph Fasano, Margo Berdeshevsky, Jane Hirshfield, W.S. Merwin, Carl Phillips, Pattiann Rogers, Pascale Petit. Too many to name of course!

I am on Joseph Fasano's third manuscript, *Vincent*, and I am unstoppable. It is extremely rare for a contemporary poet to consume my attention with such intensity. Fasano in his own words is a poet who wants to be *opened*. His voice stands firmly between the post-modern and the modern world. He is one of the rising stars of our time.

You are well known as one of the hosts of the Los Angeles radio show "Poet's Café." How did you first become involved with the "Poet's Cafe?" As a host of the program, what do you hope your audience will take away from the show?

After my initial interview with host M.C. Bruce (Mark) I was bitten by the radio bug. Hearing one's own voice, devoid of any visual presence felt very raw and liberating. I was excited about the idea of the interview because I am an inquisitive person and I believe an attentive listener. The show's wonderful developer and producer, Marlena Bond, gave me a shot at co-hosting a few shows with Mark. As it happened, he was transitioning to Northern California and it was a lot of work and cost for him to fly in every few months and conduct a run of interviews in one day, even though he was very good at it! An animated and intelligent host with a great sense of humor. He was a lawyer and musician who also happened to be an excellent poet. At first I emulated his style but they were the wrong shoes. Over time I began to develop my own rhythm. I spent hours reading and researching my guests and attempted to create a kind of time capsule (however much one can fit into 30 minutes) of the poet's life. Usually it was chronological, but sometimes the interview was about a specific book they wanted to discuss. Over time I began to include guests who did not consider themselves poets, but whose work complemented the arts, including astrophysicist, Neil deGrasse Tyson (who enjoyed delivering his astral Tweets in rhyme) and actor Julian Sands who was performing a one-man show in celebration of playwright and poet Harold Pinter. We had playwright Stephen Sachs and a few cast members from the play *Cyrano* on to talk about poetry and how sign language was such a visually aesthetic power. ASL poetry evolved from the art of sign-language storytelling. Like oral poetry, signed performance poetry uses the conventions of repetition, rhyme, alliteration, etc. to construct patterns that add emphasis, meaning, and structure to word forms. I learn so much from my guests and I hope the listeners do too.

Another hat you wear is that of co-producer of the Moonday Poetry Reading Series in California. First of all, how did the Moonday Reading Series get its start? And, what is the story behind the curious name, Moonday? What are the continuing goals for the Moonday Series as it enters its 12th year? Is anything new in the works for the Series?

Moonday has its roots on the West Side of Los Angeles. When a reading at the former Barnes & Noble at the Westside Pavilion, run by poet/dramatist, rg cantalupo, was suddenly discontinued by management in 2002, my co-host, Alice Pero resurrected the series with the help of cantalupo and poet, Anne Silver (my predecessor) at Seattle's Best in Santa Monica. Moonday moved briefly to another coffee shop, then spent eight wonderful years at Village Books in the Pacific Palisades. I came on board as co-producer in 2006 after Anne Silver passed away. When Village Books finally closed its doors, Moonday found a new home at the Aldersgate Retreat House/Buerge Chapel, also in the Palisades with a very successful run for two more years. After a brief time at the lovely Little Theater in Santa Monica, we are now at the beautiful Flintridge Bookstore in La Cañada, California where we plan to stay. The bookstore is a gorgeous new venue with plenty of outside and underground parking, a café and a lovely and well stocked poetry section. We love it there. Moonday used to be Mondays and since it was the second Sunday of the month, there was always a full moon! Anne Silver, coined the name *Moonday* and it stuck!

For nearly 13 years Moonday has held a monthly reading and at one point we were running two readings a month on both sides of the city. Alice and I have other interests but we wanted to keep the Moonday name and reading alive because our east side community depends on it so we've reduced the series to about 6 times a year which works out great. We provide a full web page for each poet, including bio, pic and poems and we've maintained a decent website presence over the years and will continue to do so. We love to discover great poets in our midst in addition to featuring some of the top names on the West Coast, including David St. John, Willis and Tony Barnstone Suzanne Lummis and so many others we will give quality newcomers a chance. We have a policy that we must both agree on the features and that has worked quite well.

Lois, we know besides everything else on your plate, your duties also extend to the *Kyoto Journal*. For readers that are not familiar with the publication, can you describe the *Kyoto Journal*? How did you become the poetry editor for the *Kyoto Journal*? What aspect of your position do you enjoy the most, and why?

First, I would like to encourage Pirene's readers to take a moment to look at our website www.kyotojournal.org. You will see immediately, the care and vision embodied by its founders. As stated on our site, "Kyoto Journal," (KJ) reflects more than a physical location. Kyoto is a place of deep spiritual and cultural heritage, and has been the measure of such things in Japan for more than a millennium. Kyoto culture has looked deeply inwards (think Zen and a host of related experiential paths) and has also drawn richly from outside, especially in relatively recent years since the Meiji modernization. Essentially, KJ is a community that transcends place, while respecting and celebrating regional and local identity. When I came on in 2007, we were still being supported by Harada Shokei, our former publisher of Heian Bunka Center who enabled KJ to produce 75 printed issues, from 1987 through 2010. Now we are completely electronic and I'm excited to share that the new KJ app will allow our subscribers to read our gorgeous issues on any of their electronic devices. Every issue is loaded with articles which reflect a vast array of Asian perspectives and our contributors cover all parts of Asia and wherever Asian people are found across the world. It also includes those of us who have had a deep connection with the Asian culture whether as long-term visitors, ex-pats or citizens.

Poetry is but a part of this great journal and we've had some greats, Gary Snyder, Arthur Sze, Brian Turner, Sam Hamill as well as many celebrated Asian poets in their original language and in translation. I'd had a poem accepted back in 2007, for issue 66. I was overwhelmed by the beauty and community of what KJ represented. I want to be involved in a literary journal that was not only aesthetically compelling but doing good works in the world. We emphasize "heart work" in KJ and that is reflected in all of us who are part of its family. As mentioned in our mission statement, the unique aspect of KJ's award-winning visual presentation is that our designers shape each story according to its individual content without relying on templates. Each article is a separate exploration and finds its own form, while often existing in a deliberate interplay with other pieces, meaning that each issue adds up to more than the sum of its parts.

There is an on-going debate about the place and power of poetry in the modern world. Why is poetry necessary in the age of hash-tags and selfies? Is it changing in some intrinsic way?

Let me start with a personal example. My encounter with the first Iraq war was like most of us – filtered through the mass media war machine. I was mortified as I watched our military strikes desiccating the city. I found all of it too difficult to process. My feelings were extremely complex and I was so angry at the arrogance of our government. What did our protests accomplish? It was said to be the biggest global peace protests before a war actually started. It wasn't until I read Brian Turner's first book, *Here, Bullet*, that I was able to have the kind of interface with war which enabled me to understand, to walk the streets of Balad as a soldier would. His poem "Ashbah" brought the futility of war to the page in the way no reporter, no photograph could do. I could see the Iraqi dead and the ghosts of American soldiers wandering the rooftops in a bleak landscape that could only be rendered by a poet, *the desert wind blowing trash/down the narrow alleys as a voice/ sounds from the minaret, a soulful call/reminding them how alone they are,/how lost. And the Iraqi dead,/they watch in silence from rooftops/ as date palms line the shore in silhouette,/leaning toward Mecca when the dawn wind blows.* I will never forget those lines.

Poetry will always be a necessary way of conveying not only the concrete images of life but what we cannot see. It gives voice to the voiceless. To slightly paraphrase Bergman, it is its own language, true to the nature of itself as it captures life as a reflection, and life as a dream. It is a way of documenting life the way a thumbprint documents a unique corporal self. It exists in the everyday even if people are not conscious of it.

Thank you so much for your time and knowledge, Lois. It was wonderful to talk to you, and to have you be a part of *Pirene's Fountain*.

And thank you so very much Elizabeth for your keen and curious questions. I really enjoyed the process. I am grateful, as ever to the whole *Pirene's Fountain* team. What you are doing in the world of poetry deserves all our support.

Allison Joseph
Rooted in Rhythm

by Lark Vernon Timmons

The difference between what's whole
and what's held, what's withheld
or revealed, what's real and what's

revelation—that's what I seek,
rest of my life spent in search

of little epiphanies, tiny sparks surging
out of the brain during the clumsiest speech.

Excerpt, "Little Epiphanies"
Published in *Valparaiso Poetry Review*

    Author of six full-length poetry publications and three chapbook collections, including her most recent release, *Little Epiphanies* (Imaginary Friend Press, 2015), Allison Joseph serves as an associate professor of

English at Southern Illinois University Carbondale. She is co-founding editor and poetry editor of *Crab Orchard Review* and director of the Young Writers Workshop—an annual summer residential creative writing workshop for high school writers.

"I write to be recorder, observer, participant, and sometimes, even judge" Joseph says. "I want to engage the world as I see it with my whole self—all of those different aspects of it."

◇

"I need sometimes to hang back in the shadows with my pen and paper, and other times to take center stage in my own creations. The trick is to know when to hang back, and when to step forward. It's a perpetual ongoing balance."

◇

"Writers have to be self-starters… to feed themselves whatever it is that will make them commit. I always say to my students, it's not all that interesting what writers do, we sit down at a computer or we write long hand. Painters get their canvases, and sculptors have all sorts of media to work with, and singers and dancers, everybody wants to see those folks. But people aren't coming over to watch a writer type…We have to follow our obsessions, even if it seems they are leading to strange places and dead-ends."

"Furtive Scribblings"

Born in London to parents of Jamaican and Grenadian heritage, Professor Joseph grew up in the Seventies and Eighties in Toronto, Ontario, Canada and the Bronx, New York—a self-described "skinny, ashy-legged girl with no particular passions; I didn't sing, or dance, or rap, or get by on my stunning good looks," she would later say—"except words were beginning to scurry around inside my brain and demand to come out."

"I hoarded pencils and pens like they were going out of style and wrote little poems in little notebooks that I hid under my bed."

Allison followed her sister to the Bronx High School of Science, one of the city's magnet schools for gifted students. Ironically, in this setting dedicated to preparing students for careers in math and science, Joseph began writing in earnest. "It was a nerdy high school," she recalls. "We were all nerds in different ways—math, debate...creative writing; all my friends were writers."

"I didn't want my Caribbean-immigrant parents to know that their first-generation daughter wasn't going to be the doctor or lawyer that they wanted. I was going to do something with these furtive scribblings—I didn't know what yet, but I knew that those little notebooks, and the books of poems I kept borrowing from the library, had something to do with what I was going to do with the rest of my life."

Excerpt(s)— *2012 George Garrett Award Acceptance Speech*

Culture Clash

As a high school senior, Joseph sought to further her education at Kenyon College in Gambier, Ohio. Its smaller population, geographical location, and reputation as a safe haven for writers seemed a good fit.

"I grew up in a black and Latino neighborhood; I went to high school with kids from everywhere in the city—white kids, black kids, Asian kids...there were 750 people in my graduating class—and I got sold on the idea of going someplace small and intimate."

In reality, she would find herself the lone female among only three black students in her freshman class at Kenyon College. The enormous culture shock and associated difficulties threatened to curtail her studies, but a determined Joseph persevered. "I learned more about editing, more about poetry, and more about helping other writers," she remembers, and now says her experience at Kenyon was not entirely unique. "I realized that a lot of people that I thought were comfortable there weren't at all comfortable."

> Let us speak. Let us talk
> with the sounds of our mothers
> and fathers still reverberating
> in our minds, wherever our mothers
> or fathers come from: Arkansas, Belize, Alabama,
> Brazil, Aruba, Arizona.
> Let us simply speak
> to one another,
> listen and prize the inflections,
> differences, never assuming
> how any person will sound
> until her mouth opens,
> until his mouth opens,
> greetings familiar
> in any language.

Excerpt, "On Being Told I Don't Speak Like a Black Person"
From *Imitation of Life* (Carnegie Mellon University Press, 2003)

Home in Carbondale

Following graduation, Joseph went on to the MFA Program in Creative Writing at Indiana University, where she first met fellow poet and editor, Jon Tribble. Their common interests and work relationship led to marriage: the two have shared a life together for over two decades.

In 1992, Allison earned her MFA and her first full-length title, *What Keeps Us Here* (Ampersand Press) was published. She then joined the faculty at the University of Arkansas at Little Rock before taking her current position at SIU Carbondale, where she and husband Jon have been teaching, editing and publishing together since 1994. Throughout their shared time in the English department, both have worked tirelessly as advocates for writers. They are founders of *Crab Orchard Review*, the Crab Orchard Series in Poetry, the Young Writers Workshop, the Devil's Kitchen Literary Festival and Reading Awards and Creative Writers Opportunities List. "All of which started," says Joseph, "with a 'What if?'"

Imagination: Engaged

"I never worry these days about whether an aspect of experience, whether it's past or present, is too insignificant to write about. I figure if it engages my imagination, it needs—requires—preservation."

Extraction

If there's a poem in you,
get it out by any means necessary—use pliers
if you must, or grab it with your bare
hands and pull, dislodging stony roots,
thorny bushes. Don't let that poem
hunker beneath your skin, unsaid,
unshed, stuck between bones or
swallowed. If it's too weak to come
out, too fluttery and unstable, feed
yourself lines from other, stronger
poems until your poem grows thick-
thighed, sable-tongued, ready to strut,
sultry, agile. If your poem is minnow-
slippery, just as quick, you must move
quickly too, casting your net wide
but not letting your poem tangle
in its nylon. No excuses when a poem
burgeons, nascent, budding on the cusp
of your lips, terrace of your tongue.
Don't let that poem sail from you,
send you a postcard later. Go get it
now, before it scurries away,
scattering words in its wake.

From *Voice: Poems*, (Mayapple Press, 2009)

What a strong impression this verse makes right off the top with its brilliant, succinct title, hard-to-match visual imagery, easy flow and inviting content. It is a present, a prescription, a poetry-writing pep talk—one I plan to commit to memory and repeat as needed.

Makeover: Esmerelda's House of Beauty

I'll need to pluck off all that eyebrow hair
then draw your brows back in—two sharp black lines.
I'll bleach your upper lip, but be aware—
this cream stings! You'll be squirming in your chair.
I'll cover up your freckles with this base,
foundation thick enough to hold a house.
I'll paint your cheeks, give color to your face,
so you'll forget about that cheating louse,
a jerk you never have to see again.
I'll perm your hair, though it is sort of limp
and fine, has more than just a few split ends,
or better yet: a wash, blow dry, then crimp.
And on your eyes, I'll brush this shimmery green,
so you'll forget he dumped you for a teen.

From *Mezzo Cammin* (Vol. 3 Issue 1)

A frequent source of inspiration for Joseph's poems is mass culture—she has called herself a "pop culture diva" who both loves and hates it. Here, she has given us a stunning glimpse of glamour as a cover for what lies beneath—a sad but entirely plausible scenario.

Sundown Ghazal

> A sundown town was a town, city or neighborhood that was purposely all-white. The term came from signs that were allegedly posted stating that people of color had to leave the town by sundown. They are also sometimes known as "sunset towns" or "gray towns." The highest proportion of confirmed sundown towns were in the state of Illinois.
> — Wikipedia

Don't show your face in a sundown town,
or forget your race in a sundown town.

What ancient shame flushes my cheeks?
Reminded of my place in a sundown town.

"How'd you get so good-looking?" said with a wink.
Old white man loves my grace in a sundown town.

Lost in a neighborhood where dogs snap chains,
my body's a dark space in a sundown town.

Shotguns, gun racks, Dixie stickers, rusted trucks.
Should I stray, armed with mace, in a sundown town?

Crimes thrive in black, white, every grade between.
Are you just another case in a sundown town?

Kink of your hair, curl of your lip,
be careful who you embrace in a sundown town.

State police, city cops, small-town hired hands.
All give chase in a sundown town.

Burned houses, riddled with junk and meth.
Hatred creeps its petty pace in a sundown town.

Black father, white mother, coffee-colored daughter.
What can love erase in a sundown town?

Rivers, tires, bodies—a confluence that cannot hide.
Hard not to leave a trace in a sundown town.

From *Heart Online* (Dec. 1, 2013); republished in *Little Epiphanies* (Imaginary Friend Press, 2015)

Joseph's use of a ghazal for "Sundown" is so effective. In simplest terms, this poetry form is composed of five to fifteen couplets in which a scheme (in this case, the phrase "in a sundown town") and refrain ("show your face," "forget your race," of my place," "loves my face," etc.) are manipulated within strict format specifications. Fixed form poetry can easily come across as stilted however, in Allison's capable hands, we as readers reap the rewards of mastery.

Sex: A Lesson

Be attentive—There are nuances
you don't want to miss: heady steam

of your lover's breath, heavy as
midnight fog, vulnerable skin

beneath an upward-tilted chin,
lips awaiting lips. Big landscapes,

little plains, twists of curves, crepe-
paper wrinkles; all need more

than furtive love, clandestine
attention. Whatever strategy

you choose—head-to-toe,
shake, then shiver, soccer stadium

shoutouts—goals are to savored,
not labored, although lovemaking

is labor, its wages not of sin,
but of surrender, of sinking in,

making room, limbs loose
long liquid, bodies fluttering

with blood-pulse and heart-thrum.
Traction meets attraction,

sweat meets sore, solace meets
satiety, all our hungers heavy

as whispers, fleeting as centuries,
slick as our wayward fingers.

From Ducts.org (Issue 34, Winter 2015)

How refreshing to read a purely sensual poem with language and images so honest the intimacy and caring are palpable—and the "coupled" lines in free verse add yet another dimension to the thoughtfully chosen words and phrasing.

Sonnet for a Good Mood

How funky can I be in fourteen lines;
how thick a groove can I lay down right here?
How bad can my ass be in these confines—
ten syllables each time seems so severe.
I'll shape this ancient form to my design,
make these iambs make you dance, move your rear.
I'll make this sonnet sweat, act refined,
just like your drunken aunt who love to cheer
her favorite Smokey song. This poem's fine
as his falsetto. Man, I'm without fear
as I strut down the page, rhythm entwined
with confidence. The beat's what I revere.
So watch now how I spin it at the end:
hands up, strut on, your psyche on the mend.

From WomanMade.org, republished in *Little Epiphanies* (Imaginary Friend Press, 2015)

I love the word-play in Allison's hip and perfectly executed sonnet. Iambic pentameter and rhyme scheme are cleverly crafted within the prescribed fourteen lines, and there is a sense of coolness, confidence and movement; a mood-boost, indeed.

A Fortunate Adventure

Joseph has called being a writer "some wicked and unfathomable combination of skill, luck, talent, drive and patience." She says "being an advocate for writers is easier, and being both has made [her] life one fortunate and amazing adventure." How fitting that on April 8, 2014, in recognition of her exemplary contribution and service to the literary community, writer's rhythm and life's rhythm merged when she received an honorary doctorate from her alma mater, Kenyon College.

Boogie is both noun
and verb for a reason, blessings
of motion due you on both page

and stage. How else will you
get your poems to flow if you
don't let your backbone slip,

if you don't subscribe to groove
theory?

Excerpt, "Why Poets Should Dance" From *Soul Train* (Carnegie Mellon University Press, 1997)

In Conversation with Allison Joseph

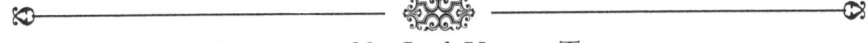

Interviewed by Lark Vernon Timmons

For those of us fascinated by the inner workings of language, would you share a bit about your poetry-writing and editing process? Are you one to jot a tag line on the proverbial napkin or bank deposit slip, tape-record notes to yourself, carry a journal and/or camera perhaps? Have you found a method that works consistently for you or does it vary, and how do you determine when a poem is finished?

> I write around the edges of everything else I do—in fits and starts. I write when I'm not teaching, editing, advising students. I build writing time into the classes I teach—sneaky! I'm constantly buying notebooks, but I don't really keep a journal per se. It varies so much.

With six full-length poetry publications to your credit, I'm interested in knowing what goes into putting together a collection. Do you begin by writing new material? What is the process for selecting work to include, and what sorts of things inform what the title will be? Has the publishing process gotten easier as you have become established as a writer?

> I often find that I'm in the midst of a book and I don't know it until it becomes fairly obvious. The book that became *My Father's Kites* began with a single sonnet. Before I knew I had a cluster of them about losing my father to diabetes. But I didn't know what the title of the book was until my former professor, Maura Stanton, mentioned that she'd seen that poem in a magazine. Light bulb went off over head—there was my title poem. The publishing process is entirely different—and separate—from the writing process. I've gotten to a point where people ask me for poems for various projects, or they want to reprint poems of mine in anthologies. It's very flattering, but I have to keep on generating material—mostly for my own creative sanity!

Allison, it is a wonderful to know that you set in motion a young writers program nearly two decades ago which continues to thrive. Please tell us your original vision for the workshop and how it has evolved/ changed/ grown across time.

> The workshop was prompted by my having attended one as a teen—the NYC Writing Project. I was also inspired by Young Writers at Kenyon, the workshop for teen writers at my undergraduate alma mater. There was nothing like that in this region (southern Illinois).
>
> The main way that the Young Writers Workshop here at Southern Illinois University has changed is through the implementation of a pedagogy class for my graduate students. My graduate students here at SIUC take a class about creative writing pedagogy, and the YWW is the practicum part of the class. It allows my graduate students to test out the ideas and exercises they've devised in a workshop setting with the high school students.

In a similar vein, I'm wondering—with texting being a primary form of written communication among teens, do you see today's young students lacking basic language skills, i.e., correct spelling, proper grammar, sentence construction, or formal writing practices? Are you able to help students establish a style of their own whether or not such limitations exist?

> The students who come to my young writers workshop may be the exception, but they are hyper-literate. They are people who grew up reading *Harry Potter.* They write novels of their own. They do not have literacy issues. It's a self-selecting group, though. We appeal to students who would seek to spend five days talking about reading and writing.

Speaking of formal writing practices, I love your poem, "Elegy for the Personal Letter" in which you compare the experience of receiving a handwritten letter to a computer-generated one. Among other things, it is a fine example of the "feeling vs sentimentality" debate—

> "I miss the rumpled corners of correspondence,
> the ink blots and crosssouts that show
> someone lives on the other end, a person
> whose hands make errors, leave traces."

How exactly do you teach your students (and the rest of us) to express sentiment without taking the "greeting card" route?

> Start small. Concentrate on the original prompting image—and build from there. Students often want to leap to writing a poem's "theme" before they've written the poem's marrow. Details enliven a poem, and so I tell students to slow down, generate them all.

It's clear you are equally adept at crafting fixed form poetry and free verse (impressive!)—Regarding your most recent full-length book, *My Father's Kites*, what factors were involved in your decision to compose poems relating to him in sonnet form?

> Since I was writing a lot about my late father, I needed some mechanism to help me control the pain, anger, and grief of loss. The search for end-rhyme in a sonnet, for example, can serve as a distraction in a way. It makes the writing of a poem—the poetic process—a bit more controlled. It was a way of mapping out the territory.

Glass Lyre Press was fortunate to have you and your husband (poet/writer and one of the founding editors of Crab Orchard Review) Jon Tribble, read at a "Lyre Live" event in the Chicago area last year. (Lovely, thank you!) Do you believe some poems are more suitable for reading aloud than others, and do you write with the intention for your verse to be read aloud?

> Some poems beg to be read aloud. My chapbook, *Voice*, (from Mayapple Press) has that theme as its basis. Those poems were all poems I had read aloud at readings, but didn't have in a collection.

Some poems, due to their length, don't readily permit reading aloud as much.

With your writing, editing and professorial duties, you (and Jon) must have a full calendar! Is writing an integral part of your day-to-day life, or are you able to set it aside from time to time? How much of your job description involves travel, and what sorts of things do you enjoy outside of your career responsibilities? Are you, like most writers, a voracious reader? Just curious, what titles are on your "want to read" list these days?

I read a lot as a teacher and editor. I don't get to read as much as I want for pleasure, especially since I've been on award panels for post-publication book awards lately. My house is full of books, some of which I've been able to spend significant time with, some of which I've had to read critically, and some of which I bought because they were curios. My house is decorated in "pile of books."

Last, not least, would you share what you have in the works currently and any plans and/ or projects you have in mind for the future? We will all look forward to seeing what comes next!

My new chapbook, *Little Epiphanies*, was published this spring by Imaginary Friend Press. Another chapbook, *Multitudes*, is forthcoming from Word Tech Communications. Also, planning my next full-length book and writing new poems as they come. I'm grateful for all the words that come my way.

Sincere thanks to Allison Joseph for sharing her time, talent and kind permissions for this feature and interview. Allison's collection, The Purpose of Hands, is upcoming from Glass Lyre Press in 2016.

Featurette

—

Jane Hirshfield

Jane Hirshfield
Ten Windows: How Great Poems Transform the World

by Linda Kim

Considered a classic of its kind, Nine Gates has been taught to students of architecture, dance, and the visual arts as well as to writers of both poetry and prose. Works of insight, wisdom and learning, these ruminations about the essential nature of art are grounded in philosophy and world literature; Jane Hirshfield's essays are meditations on life as well as poetry. One might say Hirshfield's most recent book of essays, Ten Windows, is a natural extension from her explorations of poetic craft in Nine Gates. In Ten Windows, Hirshfield welcomes the reader to delve even deeper as she speaks of lyrical craft and how the extraordinary can be found in the most ordinary of things. It is the act of picking up a rock, holding it to the light, and seeing it anew. In ten essays she elaborates on how the poetic form opens up and unfolds in a continual act of growth in an astonishing act of transfiguration that "draws from us what we did not know was there to be drawn." The experience of poetry, at how it gives voice to the voiceless and gives name to the unnameable, is an invitation to musicality and whimsical imaginings. Poetry is seeing. It is a window that catches the eye and offers a glimpse into new realities, new discoveries, and epiphanies of "unfathomable brevity" wholly suited to be "a near-weightless, durable instrument for exploring a single moment's precise perception and resinous depths." With her sparkling prose Hirshfield deepens our senses and reveals how poetry can reflect and expand on the most central issues of life, how they can transform our thinking.

The Beauty
by Jane Hirshfield

Review by Linda Kim

The Beauty is a play on perspective, on the transformative power of poetry. It invites the reader to look beneath the surface and enter greater depths. Jane Hirshfield's minimalist attention to detail, exquisite prosody, and natural musicality lends a rich texture to her work. Deceptively simple sentences and short lines betray their complexity with newly invigorated syntax, rhythm and flow. As in the short forms of poetry by Bashō and Pound, this work offers an even greater clarity of thought through its subtextual brevity. Each word imparts irrevocable impact. The preservation of a single moment interlocks with the everyday experiences of the poet who can assemble the pieces into fresh possibilities. In contemplating life and its stages, "Angular wristbone's arthritis, / cracked harp of rib cage, / blunt of heel, / opened bowl of the skull, / twin platters of pelvis—" Hirshfield shows a reverence for time's presence and absence, its lasting marks and evidence.

Hirshfield's preoccupation with time—the way it bends, its malleable qualities, the way it turns and shifts in multidimensional perspectives—makes her explorations of form, space, and memory fascinating. She gives weight and meaning to the otherwise abstract and floating. Time may be conceptual, but clocks are as physical and concrete as the images she conjures. Her juxtaposition of disparate images, as well as words that do not belong together until they do, creates strings of logic and associative lines of thought where meanings transform and transcend.

The Beauty is a demonstration of how the best poems can open and expand beyond the borders of the page, beyond expectation. Animals, plants, nature, and water become deft clay for her to shape and mold into meanings about the universality of the human experience and our ardent need for words. Her fascination with the qualities of silence, still life paintings, windows, glimpses and gazes leads to a natural foray into ekphrastic art. Inspiration is sparked by visual arts, photographs, Chinese scrolls. Consequently, there is a lightness and buoyancy to her poems that recalls the delicate calligraphy or deliberate brushstrokes of a Chinese painting in which the ink upon the canvas, the page, fades away at the edges into quieter places, rich locales for thought. Lineation is a threshold between realities: "The happy see only happiness, / the living see only life, / the young see only the young. / As lovers believe / they wake always beside one also in love."

Ultimately, Hirshfield is a champion of the peripheral and the ordinary. In *The Beauty*, one finds the sensuous and intellectual clarity similar to cinematography where a story unfolds in just a few skillful shots: "Rain fell as a glass / breaks, / something suddenly everywhere at the same time." Jane Hirshfield captures the unseen, the elusive and fraught, the beautiful and immersive. Her poetry is still life and scrutiny, movement and light. It is evocative and deeply imbued with meaning. This is a master poet's mind at work. It is a thing of beauty.

In Conversation with
Jane Hirshfield

Interviewed by Ami Kaye

To celebrate the release of two books by Jane Hirshfield this year, *The Beauty* and *Ten Windows*, we are reprinting an interview from our October 2009 online issue, where Ms. Hirshfield shares her insights in response to questions based on her essays: both a series of recent ones (published in such periodicals as *The American Poetry Review* and *The Associated Writers Programs Chronicle*) and those collected in her highly acclaimed book on craft, *Nine Gates: Entering the Mind of Poetry* (HarperCollins, 1997).

Jane, it's an honor to speak with a poet who brings such a rare and deep vision both to poems and to thinking about how poems work. Perhaps we can start by talking about the trope of "hiddenness," the subject of an essay that appeared in *The AWP Chronicle*. Early on, you quote a line from Keats's "Ode on a Grecian Urn:" "Heard melodies are sweet,

but those unheard are sweeter." You go on to comment, "Many poems hold certain of their thoughts in invisible ink." Can you tell us more about hiddenness and craft?

I've come more and more to believe in the presence and centrality of that invisible ink—or, to use a different metaphor, to believe that there is a set of hidden clockworks beneath the surface of any poem we find ourselves moved by. This is true, paradoxically, even of poems that seem to tell everything outright. A poem may seem naked or plain, but if it moves us, there will always be something else at work, under the surface of its words. This second, undertow life is what differentiates poetry from instruction manuals, journalism, or, for that matter, a diary-type journal. Good poems always travel in more than one direction. They do not soothe us with platitude knowledge, they broaden us with complication, multiplicity, permeability to the subtle, and with unexpected perceptions, gestures of language, and comprehensions.

In addition to this larger scale dimension of hidden energies in poems, there is also a set of particular craft devices that might be described as "invisible ink." One example is the deliberate choice to leave something out. A poem can convey an emotion or event's presence by walking around it, revealing its shadow, alluding without naming, pressing back against it. Poems can create meaning in the same ways that mimes create walls, tables, balls, out of thin air and their own responses. This mode of communication falls into the category of what rhetoric calls periphrasis. Think of those Chinese scrolls in which the moon is a circle left uncolored. It is simply the paper, unpainted. That is an act of visual and physical periphrasis—the ink brush touches everything but the moon itself, which is, as in the physical sky, beyond any actual touch or reach.

In more subtle ways, as well, a sense of something present but unspoken makes a poem feel not only richer, more subtle, and more tactful but also more convincingly "true," because it seems three-dimensional. What has a front, a back, an unseen interior, feels to us real. Yet another example of "invisible ink": if some emotion or event seems impossible to describe effectively, or perhaps at all, it can still be conveyed by leaping over it, going straight to some aftermath condition. You can describe a storm, or you can describe the wreckage afterward—the boat in a field half a mile inland from shore tells us most everything we need to know of water and wind. What the reader imagines in the absence of words is often more powerful than anything words could evoke, because the reader's own thoughts, associations, and experience can perfume the poem.

In the essay "Poetry and Uncertainty," which first appeared in The American Poetry Review, you allude to Keats again, this time to his idea of "negative capability" ("…. *Negative Capability, that is when man is capable of being in uncertainties, Mysteries, doubts without any irritable reaching after fact & reason.*"). The essay examines that concept in different ways. Can you tell us how uncertainty relates to poetry and its making?

It's always hard for me to summarize my essays, but the gravitational center of that one is that good poetry always includes not only knowing but also some real measure of not-knowing. Uncertainty is the basic condition of life, a condition that most of the time we try to ignore. Good poems let that essential unknowability into the room, and we are changed—our relationship to our lives is changed—by agreeing to its presence.

I'm in general wary of certainty, which tends to limit not just the imagination but also compassion. We do need to know things of course. Facts exist, and they matter. There are objective truths, at least for the purposes of daily life. Yet our certainties also create fixity and boundary in us, and a surfeit of sureness can lead to rigor mortis of intellect and heart. It's a poet's job to be vulnerable, and at risk. The subject haunts my poems as well as the essay, and has been much on my mind in recent years, raised in no small part by the seeming increase of fundamentalist beliefs in the world. Those reified beliefs' effects seem to me universally disastrous, no matter which ones or whose they are. I am aware of the irony of the seeming certainty with which I say this. But I've come to feel that nothing is more dangerous to self and others than a person sure of her or his own rightness. When I find myself adamant, in life or in a poem, I try to catch that tone, and administer a useful antidote—a question. "Is that so? Is it the whole story?" Sometimes I'll end up letting a statement stand, sometimes I'll change it, or add to it. The habit of questioning a little further is what matters—it throws open the doors to the new.

The defining gesture of a lyric poem, for me, is that its words create and then preserve, in revisitable form, some act of discovery. This means there must be some point in a poem's composition when the author cannot really know what he or she is going to say— the already known cannot be discovered. Many poems of course hold re-discoveries, refreshments of discovery. That is no less real. Some realizations or recognitions cannot be made what food producers call "shelf-stable"— they need to be created from scratch each time. The realizations I most care about are like this: they are fragile and evaporative and can only be held aloft as a hot-air balloon or soufflé is, by some active counterforce to the ordinary gravities of complacency, sleepiness, and received comprehension.

To find your way to any discovery requires exceptional attention. The mind and heart and tongue need to be free of shackles if they are to leap. The teaching motto of the Korean Zen teacher Seung Sahnim was "don't-know mind." The Japanese Soto Zen teacher Suzuki-roshi famously said, "In the beginner's mind there are many possibilities, in the expert's, only one." Then there was Sartre, who described genius as what we invent in desperate circumstance. That statement points to the necessity for heat—for the passion that causes attention and language to rise beyond their ordinary capacities and satisfactions.

To make a new poem, you need a new person. This moment's person, with this moment's needs. Otherwise, you might as well simply read one of the many great poems already written. The only reason to want to write something new is that you need to find something out for yourself, to run the old problem freshly, through your own life, tongue, perceptions, and feelings. Poetry is the antithesis of mathematics. In poetry, the old problems (love, loss, suffering, bewilderment, Wordsworth's excess of emotion, the ancient conundrums of philosophy and myth and spirit) remain perhaps constant—these things are bedrock in human life. But their solutions need to be re-found each time, and will never be exactly the same as the one found before.

I'll add one more thing. The expansions of subject matter and style in lyric poetry over the past thousand years or so are a matter of not only new persons but also of new "problems" being let in to the field of the poem. Men, for instance, did not know until quite recently that there were poems to be written about fatherhood and their children— then suddenly we find Galway Kinnell writing a poem about the birth of his son. That kind of discovery also has to do with uncertainty and not knowing. A person has to "not know" what poetry is, what belongs or doesn't belong in a poem, to bring something new into poetry. Basho had to not know that haiku were only a parlor game and amusement. Gerard Manley Hopkins had to unbind his ears from known metrics and musics. What can be found when expertise is replaced by exploration is breathtaking. But to explore, you need to venture past the edge of the already constructed map, whether physical, conceptual, or emotional.

This reminds me of what you wrote in an your earlier essay, "Poetry and the Mind of Indirection," in Nine Gates. You wrote about attentiveness, craft, and their opposite: "Craft and consciousness matter. But a poet's attention must also be open to what is not already understood, decided, weighed out. For a poem to be fully alive, the poet needs to surrender the protection of the known and venture into a different relationship with the subject—or is it the object? Both words miss—of her attention. The poet must learn from what dwells outside her conceptions, capacities, and even language: from exile and silence." Can you share with us how "knowing" and "not-knowing" balance each other in crafting a poem?

Most of the time, when we talk about craft in poems, we naturally speak of things that are able to be spoken of. We talk about what we know and what we can say. And so we say, "Verbs are stronger blacksmiths of meaning than adjectives are, yet sometimes, the plainest adjective, a color, say, can bring enormous expansion to a poem, simply by engaging the senses." We say, "Each moment of your reader's granted attention is a gift you must repay with something worthy; every syllable, every comma, must be in the poem for good reason." We say, "There are at least seven different forms of 'you,' and if you change between them mid-poem, the reader must be able to know that has happened, or will be confused." We say, "Some poems pause to look at something outside their given world; these window-moments bring light and air, volume and contrast, and can be what allows the unbearable to be fully felt."

These are the kinds of craft points I make when I teach. I teach punctuation as a form of orchestration and musical notation. I teach close reading, rhetoric, transitions. But the opposite of all this, equally important, cannot be taught; it can only be remembered and acknowledged. After a poem is written, something of what has happened outside the writer's consciousness can sometimes be named. But during the writing, the poet cannot know everything about the poem. In lyric poems, I suspect the poet often enough may not know much of anything. Not what it is about, not where it is going. The poem needs its first draft intoxication, its subversive trickster energies, its whistling in the dark, its unexpected and unfendable off pang of longing. A poem too sure of itself will have no crack for breathable air to enter, and will die for lack of permeability. Poems that are alive will have a life of their own, beyond the control of the writer. The writer's only task when that life arrives is to get out of its way.

We are the amanuenses of our poems. They dictate us. Or so it seems to me. We learn everything we can of craft so that what we know can be of service to what wants to come through us.

In yet another essay, "Poetry and the Constellation of Surprise," you wrote: "Good poems provide an informing so simultaneously necessary and elusive that they are never, it seems, taken in fully, and

can never be fully used up." Can you share this insight?

That essay began with a question I suddenly realized I had been carrying in the back of my mind: How is it that we never tire of reading a great poem? No matter how many times I've read Cavafy's "Ithaka," for instance, it has never failed to move me. The same is true of great paintings—we do not tire of them, we do not exhaust them. I thought about this for months, and finally came up with the ideas that underlie the sentence you've quoted. But it took the whole essay to spell out the recipe for elusiveness and necessity. All I can say briefly is what the essay's title says: poetry's perennial newness has something to do with discovering and then preserving, for perennial re-discovery, something surprising. This is done in the way a magician sustains the surprise of the rabbit, or the way a winding road preserves the shock of the glittering, tall city it leads to: the traveller cannot take the destination in ahead of time, because, while moving toward it, you can only see what is there, immediately around you. Poems are not lab notebooks—they are the experiment itself, which must be run completely each time, inside the reader. If a poem were some summarizable "conclusion," we would not need the poem.

We're fortunate to live in a world where we can read the literature of many cultures, first written in the author's native language. Reading works from other traditions, you've said in your essay on translation in *Nine Gates*, enriches and informs our own. In your essay, "The World Is Large and Full of Noises," you speak of the delicate balance between freedom and fidelity in translating. Could you elaborate on that thought, and also the way the practice of translation can change a writer's relationship to her own work?

I always like to begin by acknowledging that there are different philosophies of translation. Walter Benjamin famously suggested that the qualities of the original language (not only its sounds, but also its idiosyncracies of grammar, word order, and so on) should be preserved in a translation. Other translators advocate the approach I've followed in my own translations, what Octavio Paz describes as "the same effects by different means." You might at first think of these two approaches as "fidelity of surface" vs. "fidelity of sense," but any time you divide poetry up so simply, you end up in trouble—the substance and meaning of any poem is in the physical sounds it makes as much as in its ideas. Word choices, rhythms, sentence structures, dipthongs, and trochees—what other body does a poem have? Poems are not ghosts: their feet are countable, and real.

A few translators of great genius, such as Richard Wilbur, manage to convey both sound and sense quite closely. A rhymed sonnet in French can become a rhymed sonnet in English. This is less easily done, though, in languages more diverse. A Japanese poem might have no specified grammatical voice; a Chinese poem might not indicate whether its verb tense is past, present, or future. In bringing such poems into English, you almost always have to make a choice. In such cases, certain kinds of freedom *are* in fact fidelity. The same holds for cultural background information that may not be in a poem's words, but would be known to everyone in its home culture. Whether by footnote or adjective, that information needs to be given, if the reader is to have access to the full poem, and not be left standing outside a window, peering in at food you cannot eat and fire whose warmth you cannot feel. It's the translator's task to find a poem's core heat, and to carry that embering coal across time and language unextinguished

Translation is also (as you've alluded to in your question) the way that new modes and structures come into a poetic tradition. The sonnets of Keats and Donne and Millay and Gwendolyn Brooks came to us first in sonnets written in Italian. The imagism that changed American poetry so profoundly in the early 20th century came from long-standing poetic strategies of China and Japan. The Spanish poets gave American literature the "deep image" and surreal freedoms. Neruda and Ponge swung wide poetry's embrace of everyday objects. It was the translated Bible that gave Whitman his armature, his embouchement, his praise of all being. The Urdu ghazal has influenced contemporary American poetry far more than is generally realized. And that is how it should be. When new techniques of thought and feeling come into a language, if the graft takes at all, it will soon be indistinguishable as immigrant or native. The accent is recognizable perhaps for a generation, but the discovery becomes as common a heritage as bread or pizza.

For the question of translation's effects on a poet who translates, practicing translation is not unlike practicing scales—inevitably, you internalize. Certain gestures and moods cannot help but enter your own lexicon of expression. Kenneth Rexroth's essay on translating poetry is brilliant on this point, and on another as well: one reason to translate good poems, Rexroth says, is that it keeps you in such good company. For me, the year I spent translating the classical-era Japanese women's poems that became *The Ink Dark Moon* felt like a love affair—it was an exhilarating and intimate encounter; my pulses would race when I turned to the poems each week. It also became an extended exercise in openness to alternative possibility, and left me a writer with a very different relationship to revision. The experience of translating a poem seven or ten different ways, and feeling how each can be faithful to the original in its own way, is revelatory. A cook never makes the same dish twice—the salt is different, the flame is different, even the water is different. And the tongue of the cook is different. Translating poems makes clear that the same is true of words. Put two of them next to each other a thousand times, they will say a thousand slightly different things. That discovery was deeply liberating for me as a writer, and it can be learned more freely in translating than in working with your own poems: in translating, the original remains reliably there, and cannot be lost or damaged, only served.

One final question, Jane. In the chapter of *Nine Gates* called "Facing the Lion," about a poet's relationship to difficulty, pain, and "shadow" (in the Jungian sense), you wrote: "The trick then, is to let the lion into the house without abandoning one's allegiance to the world of the living: to live amid the overpowering scent of its knowledge, yet not be dragged down entirely into its realm. This is the reason Dante is forbidden pity when he looks upon the damned—to feel their fate too intimately would put his own salvation at risk. What is required is

a certain distance—made, in part, through the mind of art itself. Every poet is a Scheherazade, acceding to fate while at the same time delaying it. And Scheherazade's salvation, not unlike Dante's, is accomplished by abundance and imagination, by her offering the cruel king the one thing he cannot do without: a story worth hearing. For it is not our death the lion wants to eat, but our lives. In the difference lies one of the great source-springs of poetic power." Could you tell us more about the poet as a Scheherazade?

Scheherazade, of course, is the young woman who narrates the stories we have come to know as *The 1001 Nights*. The underlying movement of those tales, which most of us learn so young that we are unable to see them for what they are, is the story of the reassembling and cure of a broken heart and psyche. That is of course the King's—a man who, betrayed by his wife, will not risk his heart again. He decides to sleep each night with a new virgin, who is slaughtered at dawn. Many have died when Scheherazade, the King's vizier's daughter, volunteers for her turn in his bed, but with a plan—once the King has had his way with her, she begs permission to tell her younger sister one final bedtime story, which dawn interrupts. The King, who has been listening, keeps her alive for one more night, to hear its end. But one story leads to the next, each interrupted. This goes on for 1000 nights, until the King has both fallen in love with the teller and, equally important, has come to understand that his own story is not exceptional, but part of the common lot. Trickery, lust, betrayal come to all. Laughter is a saving grace. Perspective and wisdom are possible. Connection, risk, desire, and ingenuity enlarge life, anger, coldness, and separation foreclose it. And so by the time Scheherazade completes her last tale, the King has been restored to an unfractured existence by his acknowledgment that life will be what it will be for us all. Words have reawakened first his curiosity, then his willingness to live.

Poems, Robert Frost wrote, are a momentary stay against confusion, beginning in delight and ending in wisdom. That progression is a good description of Scheherazade's task—to take a person who has lost his ground of humanity and compassion, and, through the experience of moment by moment delight, through the lure of narrative skill and the evocation of life's range, absurdity, and beauty, restore him to his wisdom and wholeness.

Poems are one way we relearn the capacity to go on, no matter what happens to us in the course of a life. Scheherazade does not fear death, nor does she court it—but she risks it, she moves toward it rather than away. Her one defense against the King's ruined pride and ruinous power is a set of seductions: the seduction of well-crafted art, the seduction of human commonality, and (not to be underestimated) the seduction of her own presence, fully and vulnerably offered. All this seems to me to model something of direct use to aspiring poets.

Pirene's Fountain also gratefully acknowledges the publishers of the works and extracts in the conversation above: *The American Poetry Review, The AWP Chronicle*, and HarperCollins for *Nine Gates: Entering the Mind of Poetry*. The materials and quotations culled from various books and journals are used with the author's permission.

Reviews

Strange Theater
by John Amen

Review by Ami Kaye & Linda Kim

To fully appreciate John Amen's new book *Strange Theater* (NYQ Books), readers must first discard the familiar as the curtain rises to reveal a stage of surreal and evolving landscapes. With its startling language and strident voice, *Strange Theater* is an edgy, fresh, and groundbreaking collection. The poems in this book are small scenarios, where the cast of characters seem to have catapulted from a macabre *Cirque de Soleil* set, their enigmatic expressions casting a mysterious quality to the strange theatre of life.

Images unfold then break apart, snapped into strange alternative versions of themselves. One encounters performative realities, artifice and actuality, spectacle and deconstruction in which elements are smacked together into new definitions and original thought. The book is a question of identity, of naming a collage of disparate parts. It is the genre-mashing juxtaposition of the mundane with the fantastical, of robots and machinery set side-by-side with the fantasy of castle, giants, kingdoms, and dragons, a mocking foil to our fumbling bipedal follies.

Strange Theater boldly plays with ideas, breaks rules, and breaches boundaries. Sometimes only a sly wink is necessary, as in "bird in a bottle" (p. 31), which acknowledges the absurdity of gleaning universal truth in poetic fragments of thought. Amen pokes fun at how serious poetry can be and how the genre can become rigid under the weight of its own yoke when it is called Literature. After all, "a bird in a bottle / is sometimes just a bird in a bottle" (p. 32).

Amen has a striking way of upping the stakes. He intuitively understands how to manipulate emotions through escalation and emotional beats. In "untitled #7" (p. 40) he orchestrates a comedic tone and image, "our planet's the psych ward of the solar system / then again I can see the moon from my toilet" only to abruptly turn the corner. The ensuing mood whiplash is eerie and stark, and the previously established lighthearted tone disintegrates instantly, "the funniest thing isn't always funny / or at some point ceases to be funny / I show my teeth while I laugh / reminds me of being tickled by a molester when I was 8." There is the realization and let down when faith no longer supports one's need, "stumbling towards an altar / no longer there/ you grab for pages in the sky" (p. 16). An underlying anxiety threads through the narrative, an awareness of things getting more difficult as in "self- portrait on 71st" (p. 27):

> I'll testify
> each fear grows more terrible than the last
> each rope extends deeper
> each stone takes longer to punch the water's surface

Section one of the book informs our understanding of the dynamics in the following section, but there is a reason the title of the book is lifted from its middle hinge poem, "Strange Theater" (pp. 56-65). It acts as a precarious ledge for readers to teeter on, continually revising all prior understanding of the book. The direction irrevocably shifts with this poem. Now we begin to infer the cosmic horror that is the next preoccupation of the book—infinite realities, looping time, the futility of changing the script, how it never ends, and how one never breaks free. Existential despair is a self-perpetuating loop. The conflation of theater with filmic settings allows for this scenic buildup.

The environment of *Strange Theater* morphs into something darker with every new insinuation. The closer we get to Section two, the more mature the content becomes. The surrealist traumas and scenes previously hinted at now overtly visualize divorce, slaughter, mental hospitals, cancer, abuse, rape, miscarriage, suicide, addiction, crime, and flawed institutions. Religious comfort, solace, and succor rip apart in the face of anguish, disillusionment. God is found to be remote, cold and distant as a machine. He is the "famous impresario / no longer active in the sky" (p. 45). Section two takes strands of religious bitterness from the preceding section and hardens them into a razor sharp edge. After all, what kind of all-powerful cosmic being would allow his creations to suffer such pain and tragedy? The Jewish programmer of "1942" becomes reduced to nothing with "lines of code dispersing like chemtrails" (p 71). Genocide didn't end with World War II.

Strange Theater abounds with fractured glimpses of disjointed realities. It delights in subverting expectations. Like Dali's melting clocks in his "Persistence of Memory," time itself is fluid, and lends itself to unfamiliar dimensions of experience. John Amen's strange theatre is floodlit by a brutal, unflinching honesty. He offers a unique insight into how people look for meaning in a world plagued by the shifting seismic plates of technological invasion and isolation, how they grasp for perspective and hope in this rapidly evolving world. His vision provides a necessary, if disturbing exploration of the forces that shape and thwart our lives,

you say *each scorpion represents*
a sin or virtue you name each accordingly
if you're stung enough times
balance can be restored
the world return to what it was
before you can't remember.

Love is a Burning Building
by J.P. Dancing Bear

Review by Elizabeth Nichols

    As with all collections of love poems, J.P. Dancing Bear's Love is a Burning Building strives to say something new on a topic about which much ink has been spilled. In this, Love is a Burning Building triumphs, breathing new life into the realm of love poetry. While it is cliche to say that love transforms the way in which the lovers see the world, Bear's poetry goes further and makes love a force that bends the very fabric of reality: the "world" becomes "a round of calendars," the "sun" a "lemon slice," and love a "burning building." Bear's poems possess a dreamlike quality, as if each moment in human life is spent in a beautiful waking sleep:

From "Disintegration of the Persistence of Memory"

> the soft clocks are melting: while the universe breaks: down to atomic
> sub-particles: the lip of the ocean is peeling back: old paper curling:
> layer
> after wave: fish know not where to school: even after timepieces
> convert:
> to a liquid state:

The reflection on Salvador Dali's famous surrealist painting of the same name mirrors the collection as a whole, which takes the images of life and arranges them helter-skelter. Like glass beads in a kaleidoscope, these images jumble and glint chaotically until they are knit together by the poems' careful structure. All of Bear's poems, like "Disintegration," are punctuated from colon to colon, creating a series of interconnected images that at once flow together and yet remain distinct. This technique is especially powerful for describing love: it reflects an emotion that is jarring, comes in starts and stops, and yet burns and endures.

Bear's poetry often finds a fixed point of contemplation by using a central image, pulling into its orbit an emotional weight greater than itself. One such poem is "Dog in the World," which uses the image of a dog to describe a world's worth of joy, effervescence:

From "Dog in the World"

> you say there is something about a dog: that reflects the rest
> of the world: in its perked up ears: wagging tail: ready for the
> next moment's joy: certain it will come: and the dog reflects
> the eagerness of the dog: off every appendage…

Joy builds on joy, gathering around the dog and building into revelation. This one, small moment in time resonates across a lifetime. The dog becomes a symbol of happiness: "Its coat is one of mirrors: a million / moments of happiness all within one moment." And the reader, too, is pulled into the orbit of the dog: "you cannot help but / smile: which is reflected back at you: from so many different parts: and / angles of the dog." It is as if Bear's poetry interprets dreams, translating the image of a happy dog into a moment that reveals the essence of joy; of unconditional, ecstatic love.

Similarly, the titular poem of the collection uses an extended metaphor to describe love. Fire becomes love, creating heated emotions that consume the lovers:

From "Love Is a Burning Building"

>...and now this fire: this urgency: you run through the
>flames: wrapped in a sheet: through trapped billowing smoke: you bound
>the stairs: you know the door: you kick it in: you pull her body into your
>arms: carry her out into the street: as you've always known you would:
>when you first struck the match: so many weeks before

The burning building is an extended metaphor for the relationship between the two lovers. When, at last, emotions run high, things come to a head and the two come together. But this is not a random act. It was a lover that first struck the match that set two lives alight. Even as the flames turn the building into a pyre, the lovers still have agency. They choose the blaze, and by extension make love a risk that is worth taking. Ultimately, *Love Is a Burning Building* will do to the reader what the fire does to the lovers: transport them to a world of heady surrealism, where metaphors and poetry are the only ways to describe what there are "no words for." *Love Is a Burning Building* beautifully reaffirms that love's language is poetry, capturing something that is as difficult to grasp as a flame.

Temporary Champions
by Darren C. Demaree

Review by Elizabeth Nichols

In Temporary Champions, Darren C. Demaree gives a voice to fighters, translating the blows of the boxing ring into powerful lines of poetry. Demaree not only describes the act of boxing—its intricacies and inherent spectacle—but also fleshes out the inner conflicts taking place in the hearts and minds of the fighters and their audience. Temporary Champions redefines the words "fight," "fighter," and "audience" so that they not only apply to the context of boxing, but also to the society that consumes the spectacle of a violent sport. "When worlds / are built out of collision," explains the speaker in "Round 1," "the violence of a collision / is how we begin to dictate what matter is, / what will matter to us...." In other words, there is something more at work in the world of boxing than just punches and bells: something vital can be learned about the human experience from boxing.

In the poem "Because I Tried to Like It Very Much," Demaree explores why boxing matters to the fighters and the audience and, therein, why the valuation of boxing is problematic. The poem's speaker describes his mixed feelings about the high-contact sport:

From "Because I Tried to Like it Very Much"

> ...I watch it now,
> almost every day, knowing
> the last two rights are coming,
> knowing the canvas will double as a coroner's bag,
> knowing that my vision
> of what a man really is
> can be found in round thirteen
> but learning that I am
> not much of an enthusiast
> for what it is men can do.

Here, boxing matters to the fighters and the audience because it is a test of masculinity. The speaker acts as a poetic sociologist, studying boxing as a cultural event that affects its participants and spectators. The speaker begins by commenting on the curious fact that even before the fight begins the audience knows that a fighter could be fatally injured by his opponent. The speaker is unnerved by the fact that this risk is acceptable in exchange for the excitement of a boxing match. At the same time, the speaker understands that boxing is one way in which the traditional definition of masculinity—"what a man really is"—is reinforced. The limits of the human body are tested in "round thirteen," bringing the proof of masculinity to a bloody, black and blue conclusion. The speaker is unsettled by what men can do to one another in the name of being men.

In boxing, the traditional definition of masculinity is made into a violent spectacle, which brings to light a problematic aspect of the sport. "If you re-watch film of the victor," the speaker concludes in "God-Hungry, Harsh, Magnificent," "if you watch it a third time, / you will see only how bloody he is / & even wrapped in joy, his body / is unhappy with the current trials / & after that, only elegy exists." At the end of the trial of masculinity, the only things left are injury, pain, and possible death.

In fact, Demaree's collection is haunted by the death of a boxer. "Kim" is a Korean boxer killed in the ring, and the collection devotes several poems to trying to understand his death. In Demaree's poems, Kim's death affects not only his family (as described in "Death Trickles through Every Family Crack"), but also the audience and, by extension, the society that consumes the spectacle of boxing. In the "The Crowd #38," the speaker describes the aftermath of Kim's death in the ring:

> ...when they carried Kim out on the
> stretcher they carried all of us
> with him. We woke up in the
> hospital, full of confessions.

The speaker assigns the guilt of Kim's death not only to the brutality of the sport, but also to the audience that pays for, and demands boxing. The "confessions" of the audience suggest a societal culpability in Kim's death that the speaker of the poem finds inescapable and inexcusable. In addition, the "confessions" that the audience wakes up with in the hospital are like the "concussions" that a boxer wakes up to after the fight. In only a few lines, the audience becomes the injured boxer. But, in a final reversal, it is the audience that wakes "up in the hospital:" an experience that Kim is robbed of by death. In the end, the value of boxing and the value of a human life are weighed and measured, and when the scale tips in favor of boxing, the audience and the reader are left reeling—left wanting for reason in a senseless death.

All that is left in the ruins of the sport of boxing are temporary champions. Kim is the obvious temporary champion, because he reached for glory and only caught a glimpse of it before death stole it from him. But, the audience is also a temporary champion, vicariously reveling in the spectacle of boxing, and sharing in the triumphs and tragedies of the ring. The audience waits "in the drift of sand for another man to lift them past / the bowled stadiums, past the collection of races, of / so many examples of human wreckage, all stomping / to overtake the arcade of the hymnal." In *Temporary Champions*, poetry elevates boxing to a mythic status: Kim becomes a tragic hero that is defined by a physical test—a tragic hero whose death says volumes about society. Ultimately, Demaree makes the reader recognize that the boxing ring is an ugly microcosm of the struggle of human existence, and that the reader himself is a temporary champion in that struggle.

Dreaming of the Rain in Brooklyn
by Howard Faerstein

Review by Elizabeth Nichols

Howard Faerstein's *Dreaming of the Rain in Brooklyn* leaves the reader awash in poetry petrichor, memories with all the senses and emotions thoughtfully engaged in poetry. It is as if vital memories collected as alluviate at the bottom of the soul's deep-seated rivers, and Faerstein panned through it to find the shining, golden sparks of the past. Much like novelist Marcel's Proust's madeleine moment—in which a bite of the madeleine transports the protagonist back into a vivid memory that comprises all the actions in the novel *In Search of Lost Time*—in Faerstein's collection, the reader is held rapt in a world of dream, memory, and poetry. Faerstein's gorgeous language sustains the living dream, letting the reader examine the most secret parts of himself, and others. When the reader dreams of the rain in Brooklyn with Faerstein, he finds beauty in the past, and meaning in the present—life is savored, appreciated anew through poetry.

In "Longing," the speaker aches for loved ones lost to time. As memories consume him, the speaker imagines actions that he might have taken to change the past. The speaker's regret is tangibly bittersweet, punctuated by the sound of "jazz," the taste of "malteds," and the touch of an "embrace:"

From "Longing"

> I want my mother back, smoking at our kitchen table.
>   She could finish the stories of her youth in the Springfield bakery
>   and after I scream Shut up already Enough
>   I'll blot her tears with my parched lips.
>
> I want my brother back on the handball court on Colonial Road
>   and after I call do-over and finally beat him,
>   we'll race to Pop G's,
>   order malteds, my treat.
>
> I want my father back on the 4th Avenue bus.
>   Lurching past tenements we'll drink sweet Scandinavian liqueur
>   and after I fling the schnapps in his face,
>   then tell him the damage wasn't lifelong, I'll embrace him.
>
> I want it all back
> because it was all so botched.
> But that's longing
> and longing isn't love.

This longing is not idyllic, but conflicted. The speaker struggles with the jarring discordance between the reality of the past, and the healing actions-not-taken in his dreams. Faerstein's speaker taps into universal feelings: the should-have, could-have dones that torture the human soul. The poem captures the visceral need to fix the mistakes of the past—a need achingly repeated by the speaker in each stanza—"I want," "I want," "I want," "I want." The speaker's memories occupy the gray space between dream and nightmare, for they do not absolve of him of guilt, but only serve to underscore reality: to emphasize the painful truth that "longing isn't love." In these reimaginings of the past, there is a very human selfishness at work: to fix what cannot be mended, to take back what is lost. Faerstein pens life in all its ugliness, and paints the human in all his flawed beauty, capturing his sore, full heart.

Other poems in Faerstein's collection do not leave the reader on so solid a footing of images. In "Meditation on a Dream Unrecalled," the speaker disorients the reader, describing a thing that defies dimensions, eschews definition: loss. The emotion of the dream lingers, but the images fade away as consciousness takes hold. Here, the speaker uses the fragments of the dream to plumb the depths of loss, and to make sense of the intangible:

From "Meditation on a Dream Unrecalled"

> Loss has no effacement.
> It flares with unremembered light.
>
> On the artist's white canvas,
> like an amputee's phantom pain,
> absence suggests shape,
>
> a boundary between two worlds:
> the splash of phantasm and bludgeoning of the real.
>
>   If I call up carefree night's geometry
> with its colonies of the dog-toothed violets in dappled dark,
> it's the after-image of poems,
> of trout lilies taking seven years to flower.
>
> I'd swear there was the briefest image of blue space,
> goats among fragmented stars.
>
> And then while legs orbited silhouettes of elms,
> goats vanished from an impossible sky—
>
>   once it began
>   it began ending—

> only house painters left,
> climbing ladders,
> gessoing whispered stars.

Loss cannot be expunged from the heart, only wrestled with on canvas, in poems, in dreams. The meaning of "blue spaces," "goats," and "house painters" eludes the speaker, but the images linger in the gray matter of his mind like ghosts, "after-images," that startle the senses like *déjà vu*. With potent imagery and simile, the reader is made to understand what loss feels like even if the whole of its shape falls through speaker's grasp like the grains of the sandman. In the end, the poem attempts to make the intangible tangible, transmuting the haze of the dream into the ink of written word.

Faerstein's collection also comments on the poets and poetry itself. He does so with a critical, and insightful eye—aware that as he describes other poets, he is also describing himself, a poet. The reader learns that poets succumb to the to allure of dreams:

"Even the Dog Took on Vulnerability"

> And the poets, too, how facile
> when they write of thrushes
> gaunt, arthritic, or especially terrible.
> Don't believe them. It's only a flourish.
>
> They're thinking of themselves,
> of their parents' reflections in the mirror
> before sleep overtakes them
> and they dream in the dumb
>
> contrivance of words.
> Waxwings don't perish of old age.
> They crash into power lines by Monte Vista,
> fall in the hedgerows, picked off
> by the dog running loose,
> smother in the slick that oils the shallows.

> People sicken in the late winter,
> ask for blessings from fly monks & high-heeled priests.
> Better to travel the flyways
> between scar tissue & survival.
>
> Land in their own sweet Spring.

    The speaker injects a cold reality into the realm of metaphors and creative language. The death of the waxwing may sound beautiful in stanza, but the reality is far darker: death by "power lines," "hedgerows," "dogs," and oil spills. The speaker asserts that it is misleading to wax poetic—to live in a dream conjured by the "dumb contrivance of words." Instead of asking "for blessings" from religion, instead of seeking a salve for sickness, it is better to suffer the scars and survive to find one's own "sweet Spring." A poet, argues the speaker, will not ignore the complexity of life, but instead acknowledge it, and find its beauty, its poetry.

    Faerstein's collection immerses the reader in a waking dream, reflecting on memory, poetry, and the human. *Dreaming of the Rain in Brooklyn* is a collection rich with imagery, and critically contemplative. Faerstein does not gloss over the complexity of life, its ugliness, with pretty poesy. Instead, Faerstein shows the reader the power of his own dreams: the power to uplift, fulfil, deceive, and discover the self. Ultimately, Faerstein's *Dreaming of the Rain in Brooklyn* reveals that dreams are the mind's poetry, and that poetry is the language of dreams.

Numinous
by Leila Fortier

Review by Elizabeth Nichols

In Leila A. Fortier's *Numinous*, poetry is molded by the will of the poet, by the force of her subject. Fortier's collection is a delightful example of concrete poetry, of poems shaped to reflect the contents of the lines. Fortier's concrete poetry adds another dimension to the reading of her work. The reader is struck by the shape on the page, guided by the unique flow of the words that are arranged with the same precision as dots of color in a pointillist painting. As the title of the collection suggests, spirituality informs Fortier's work, lending its ecstasy to her poetry and her painting. In fact, Fortier is the artist behind the painting that graces the cover of *Numinous* and each painting on the chapter pages therein. *Numinous* is a prolific work that stirs the spirit, exuding mysticism and poetic vision.

In "~Monsoon Emotion~," sentiment overtakes the speaker, soaks her to the skin with the rawness of her feelings. The speaker's deep-seated passion releases a torrent in her heart, flooding her senses with longing. The poem's shape invokes images of water: a raindrop, a waterfall, a fountain. Further, the shape of the poem carries an emotional gravity, drawing the reader down into the churning whirlpool that is the speaker's psyche:

From "~Monsoon Emotion~"

I
Went
Away so that
I could be made
Whole within Your
Universe~ Somehow
I returned broken~
What is this digression that leaves me so naked and
Recluse? I am now a landslide of emotion from
The monsoon You released in me~ There is
No glass to contain this ocean~ This
Cascade that submerged my
Tireless flame~ Lost
Within Your
Waves

Note that the "You" in the poem is capitalized, signaling that the object of the speaker's affection is more than just a lost lover. The "You" in the poem is spirituality charged, denoting a higher power. The speaker's emotion, then, is spiritual ecstasy. This spiritual consumption leaves the speaker naked, overwhelmed by the deluge of emotion in her soul, and the power of spirit.

Numinous lets the reader fall into a state of serenity, wrapping the reader in "clouds," in sublime imagery. In "*-Fallen-*," the speaker leads the reader in poetic yoga, breathing in the beauty of the written word. This time, the speaker is connected to the higher power—"*You*—" and finds peace:

From "*-Fallen-*":

    I have
        Fallen into You ...
            Wrapping myself
                In Your vaporous
                    Clouds if only
                        Just to linger ...
                            To share in
                                Final breath-
                                This single
                                Eternal
                            Bury into me ...
                        As I have come
                  Into You- Sleep
              Within me
            That I may feel
        Your waking ...

Here, the shape of the poem is a physical inhalation: a filling up of the spirit. But, it is also the "*Final breath*" that the speaker takes, indicating that the speaker is dying. The speaker and the higher power, "*You*," are joined at last in death: "*Sleep / Within me / That I may feel / Your waking* ..." In this death, however, there is no fear. Peace greets the speaker, guiding her to "*Sleep*" with a gentle, omnipotent hand

Finally, in the titular poem of the collection, Fortier's creative language is at its most potent. The speaker in "~Numinous~" casts the "clippings of her paper-mâché / Heart~" upon "Salmon skies," and finds her visage celestially refracted. Her soul quivers at the realization of a divine power—at the source of the "hush of white light" that gives her spirit a sacred, prismatic glow:

From "~Numinous~":

> I
> Am the
> Love that dares
> Not speak its name~ The
> Quill-tip tongue of effervescent
> Ink~ The emptied cup of "i" with
> Overflowing eyes~ For no such
> Words will part my trembling
> Lips unless anointed by
> Your haunting
> Sound
> The
> Quivering
> Echo within the void~
> This fragile benediction that
> Cast clippings of my paper-mâché
> Heart~ Scattering gold leaf against
> Salmon skies~ I disperse myself from
> The internal Mecca; explosive against
> The pleroma of heaven's canopy~ To
> Be some kind of weightless gravity
> That knows no perimeter save for
> Your face~ For I would wreck
> Myself against the weight
> Of any blasphemy
> Or earthly
> Thing
> Just
> To
> Reach
> You~ For
> I am filled with the
> Immediacy of all my lives~
> The numinous fragmentation attuned
> Only with Your imperceptible hush of white light

The shape of the poem is reminiscent of a Grecian urn, or the spine of a candelabra, giving the poem a symbolic weight. The poem references Islam with "Mecca," Gnosticism with "pleroma" and Hinduism and Buddhism with the concept of multiple "lives," or rebirth. Thus, the speaker is a part of a universal spirituality that celebrates the human. All earthly boundaries have been lifted away from the speaker, and she is at home in a new spiritual universe. With Fortier as a poetic guide, the reader experiences this spiritual universe and discovers the Numinous capacity of the human spirit.

Paradise Drive
by Rebecca Foust

Review by Elizabeth Nichols

Rebecca Foust dedicates her chapbook, *Paradise Drive*, to "pilgrims everywhere and in every time." If it were any other collection, this dedication would seem like an empty boast. But, *Paradise Drive* lives up to its dedication, and dares to push beyond the standard limitations of a poetry chapbook. *Paradise Drive* offers more than just an assortment of poems with a common theme. Instead, the reader is privileged to meet Pilgrim, a character that would be just as at home in the pages of Dostovesky's *Notes from Underground*—with its isolated protagonist—as she is in the stanzas of Foust's poetry. For readers unfamiliar with Dostoyevsky's 1864 classic, the novel is considered one of the first existentialist works, grappling with the anger and confusion resulting from a meaningless, absurd, and even cruel, world. Dostoyevsky's protagonist reacts to his harsh world by retreating underground, and shares his observations and bitter feelings with the reader. Foust's Pilgrim is the spiritual successor to Dostoyevsky's protagonist. She, too, finds that the only way to cope with, and exist in, a cruel world is to retreat from it. The reader experiences the dark reality of modern life through Pilgrim, and is left searching for hope in a world where dining with the seven deadly sins is common place.

When first introduced to Pilgrim, the reader learns that she is on a "quest," a "seeker" in a long line of seekers. In the poem "Why Pilgrim," she also takes on all that the word pilgrim embodies: its hopeful, searching idealism, and its dark past of colonialism and genocide. This duality, "good and bad," embodied in the word pilgrim, is a microcosm of the collection as a whole. Pilgrim's inner world, her tormented psyche, is writ large through poetry as she tackles the inequities of human life:

From "The Seven Deadly Sins Overheard at the Party"

2. Pride Bickering With Envy
   ...And the 4th-grade class tour
   of that chicken-farm-cum-abattoir
   is not why I'm vegan; no, my birdseed-
   and-twigs look good next to what you're not
   eating." Nearby, Pilgrim, struck by the thought
   that not all get to choose portion control,
   or can afford organic food, thinks how elite
   it all is. Then thinks again: wait
   —isn't it also elite—just—to eat?

Like the underground man, Pilgrim cannot conscience the gross discrepancies in human life: the glitter of the rich versus the gaunt forms of the poor. She cannot stomach the banality, the falseness, of the "bright party" when crises rage on around the world. Whether or not the seven deadly sins are just constructions of Pilgrim's own mind— her own faults personified—or amassed representatives of all human fallacy, the "bright party" is nonetheless a critical tool for Pilgrim with which to have an open discourse with the darker aspects of humanity.

Pilgrim admits in "Real Housewives" that "it's not easy, being a good hostess / to all Seven Sins en masse." In fact, Pilgrim relishes retreating into her own private sanctuary, "hiding out / with a book while the bright party sparkles / elsewhere." She believes that being hidden away from the world is another kind of freedom in and of itself. But, someone is always knocking at her door: the world finds a way to flood in despite her "dead-bolted" door. "Meanwhile, Elsewhere" is one such poem in which the reader gets to see snippets of the outside world through Pilgrim's eyes, as if she opened her locked door just a crack to let news of the world peek in:

> A boy whose name I cannot now recall
> in the john with his MK48
> did not come out.
>
> Zip him in his body bag; toss in
> his scarred wrists and the long, long list
> of other un-nameds; God forbid we see
> that shit—we'd have to admit it exists.

Horror and shock are potent in Pilgrim's voice as she describes the bleak, painful reality of the soldier with hidden wounds. She lashes out in anger at the blind eye society willfully turns to such suffering. Horror and shock are potent in Pilgrim's voice as she describes the bleak, painful reality of the soldier with hidden wounds. She lashes out in anger at the blind eye society willfully turns to such suffering. With such darkness eating away at Pilgrim throughout the collection, the reader, too, is left feeling like Pilgrim: enough, enough, no more—leave me in my room of books, alone to converse with the sins in my heart.

"Je Est un Autre." The title of the poem is a famous quote from the poet Arthur Aimbauld, which translates as "I is someone else," or "I am an other." Rimbauld's quote concerns the constructed self, or the persona that one wears outside that is contrary to whom one is on the inside. Foust's poem deals with this duality in a startling way:

From "Je Est un Autre"

> At that night's party, it happens. You meet
> Someone you like, very much.
> What a relief not to be
> all alone, how wonderful to agree
> on so many things! When you raise a hand
> to your hair, though, they catch the light

> your own rings. Yes, it's a mirror and—shit—you
> talking into it. A zero sum game,
> and there you are, inside the gilt frame.

Pilgrim does not recognize herself—could not see beyond her own sense of constructed self her fabricated persona. This is very troubling for the reader, as it raises questions about one's sense of self. Is the reader, too, blinded by his own construction, unable to see past a veneer into the truth? If we are all at the "bright party," blinded by the glittery veneer of our constructed selves, deaf to the suffering outside the party, and conversant with sin, human existence is dark. Is there any hope for Pilgrim in Foust's poetic vision of the world? Or, must the reader live like Pilgrim in order to see the truth: shut away, alone, a la Dostoyevsky's underground man?

No. In the midst of this darkness, Pilgrim gives the reader the best advice she has for living in an antithetical world of bright parties and war:

From "How to Live, Reprise"

> ...All you can do, Pilgrim decides,
> is keep asking the questions.
> Admit when you're wrong. Go on
> for the kids, especially the kids
> you have personally caused
> to be brought into the world.
> As far as you can, regardless,
> clean up your own mess.
> Do not use bleach in every load.

Foust's poetry reveals a story jam-packed with life, condensed and potent with human triumph and fallacy. The reader comes to care about Pilgrim, because—in the end—the reader is also a pilgrim on the human journey, conversing with sins, and reveling in or hiding from "the bright party" of the world: a world rife with illusions of grandeur and comfort, and laden with conflict and suffering.

Teaching a Man to Unstick His Tail
by Ralph Hamilton

Review by Ami Kaye

Ralph Hamilton's *Teaching a Man to Unstick His Tail* from Sibling Rivalry Press (2015) is a marvel of fresh insight, sensuality and elegance which delivers poem after poem of sweeping beauty and emotional resonance. This collection addresses the spectrum of love, and its inescapable coupling with pain. It is an amalgam of wit and sophistication, of the erotic and metaphysical, which strongly recalls John Donne's work in a more contemporary context. In *Teaching a Man to Unstick His Tail* the reader encounters vulnerability and enduring strength—a compelling combination—in passages of great lyric beauty.

Universal themes are embedded in different formats of love and loss. Hamilton's varied speakers have suffered many blows, but they are all searching for resiliency and contentment. The enigmatic phrasing of the book's title, *Teaching a Man to Unstick His Tail*, can only be clearly understood in light of nearly a hundred poems. In "Obedience School" (P. 99) the consequences of losing hope and yearning to return to a simpler, happier time is exemplified by a dog: "Still his tail thump-thumps / for another treat. It's ludicrous / his hope, though it's my aspiration / too—learning to sit, stay, to offer my belly unguarded, lick the soft / pink lipstick below my tail without shame or compulsion, to wag / as if

I believe the world waits / eager with one more bone." This image then becomes the collective desire of the book's speakers: to lift the tail up, to heal, to return, to be complete once more.

This theme is hinted at within the very first and last poem of the book, which are both offset in their own specific sections, creating a narrative throughout the book. The stark difference between the before/after states emphasizes whatever death, ending, or loss the speaker is illuminating. The fallout from emotional trauma, the reverberations of a broken relationship, heightens the painfulness of any subsequent yearning. Yet even hope proves fragile in the face of reality. The speaker's doubts emphasizes love's tendency toward uncertainty instead of absolutes. "With(out) Him" (p. 42) shows the conundrum of needing someone more than he needs you. It ruminates further on the pain of unrequited love and the difficulty in needing others to define the self. Yet the fixation on the fluidity of the beast, of how rhinoceros and barracuda entwine into one, taps into the poet's understanding of how the lines between human and beast blur, where the fantastic and realistic mingle. Even the parenthetical embedded in the title itself hints at these two realities, this potent mix of possibility that simultaneously does and doesn't exist. It is the ultimate paradox of love: which is more painful? To be with, or without the beloved? "Without him I'm lost. Like water, he's boundless. I drink him like air."

In some poems the innocence of childhood is contrasted against the disillusionment of growing up. "How the Planets Maintain Orbit" (p. 93) bridges the book's overall theme of broken relationships with the understated tension of childhood/adulthood. In the "mother" poems the speaker struggles to reconcile the child having to become the caretaker. Bitterness, shame, and weariness bleed from these lines: "*Was your mother always like this?* / the nun without habit asks. I think, *Before / she lost half her brain?*—but mutter lamely, / *She's lonely.* I'm ashamed of myself, / ashamed I lied. *Yes, Sister,* I should have / said, *Like every body ever born.*" These mother poems are unique in that they depict one of the few nonsexual relationships in the book that nonetheless explore the complexities of love and the duties that accompany it.

Relationships are deconstructed while the nature of love is dissected; the speakers all wish to understand where they have failed. The lines of "I can't sleep, you said before you bought / the new bed. Now we're boxers in opposite / corners" from "Spooning" (p. 40) depicts an unexpected turn in a relationship. "As beds grow bigger, our union/ shrinks, both so damned fat we text each other / across wastelands of thousand-count Egyptian thread." Hamilton not only displays unusual insight about relationships, he also shows technical mastery in a dazzling burst of various forms, such as the centos and semi-centos scattered through this book. "Idyll" (p. 59) is a fine example of Hamilton's deft crafting. The vital imagery in its few lines unleashes a strong current of emotion which is echoed in other poems such as Sonnet I (p. 27), "...no such thing as a breakdown not this day / they believe this   not me / so he digs   it hurts   and the dog / days come   littered with soups / cigarette butts   the heavy innocence / of childhood   marvelous dirty days dressed / in newspaper   wan as pale thighs/ aching to be fucked   it hurts   so he digs/to the big promise of emptiness   coffee   my arms"

"Pentimento" (p. 15) speaks volumes about how we grapple with loss, how small, insignificant things suddenly take on meaning, and affect us. In this piece, the speaker ruminates on his loss, thinking back to paintings that no longer adorn the wall of a shared living space: "Now certain walls gawp / oddly blank as if we'd never noticed / something was missing..." The poem ends with a delicately powerful punch, "But absence has breath, / has bones, a hue, your scent in / silence still moist on the stairs." The yearning apparent in this poem bleeds into "Stephen Hawking in Love" (pp. 23-24) in which the speaker attempts to distance himself from the confrontational sting of emotions. Early lines from this poem reveal this tendency: "If flesh is a field & desire a force, / Unified Theory holds that bodies / mediate love, though fiction prefers / hearts as the medium of fusion." The preoccupation with the body is in full force, a fixation based upon the theory that physicality can reveal interiority. Hamilton is skilled at pulling diction and concepts from non-art related fields, and then repurposing them into lyric philosophies. His associative logic of words and images are made even more eloquent with terminology and unique diction from other fields like astrophysics, biology, and medicine; in this way he can create fresh, original sentiments and observations.

In "Earthsong" (p. 92), the recounting of a suicide grips the reader with shattering emotion, enthralled by its dark and exquisite beauty:

>   Perhaps the music
> still hadn't ceased as she eased the car
> inside her garage then lowered the door
> —listening—let the motor lull: Found,
> perhaps, the shadows there soothing,
> found Mahler's dark-soiled song
> enfolding her close, found air, her
> tongue, tasting of loam, tasting of silt—
> sound filling her body with nightblue
> drift, filling her lungs with alluvial
> root—calling, calling—her heart
> beyond surfeit, so full of deep
> bloom—calling her—so suddenly
> full of earth's rapt green hum.

Even with the emotional intensity inherent in this book, a lively sense of humor pervades Hamilton's writing, as in these lines from Bird Life (p. 61): "We quail, we lark, we / snipe, we brood. Hence queer / old hens—forgive me, same- / gendered fowl—require more / than cocks and much more / than good lays to make life / gay together." In other poems, a fragile vulnerability is conveyed through a series of gorgeous images: "Your Soft Throat," a semi-cento: "I want / to give / of light the silver / young sticky leaves / quick sparrows / whipping their wings."

Hamilton's mastery over form, the way he steers narrative and drives interiority, playing with couplets, sonnets, staggered lines, prose poems, and even mid-line space in lieu of punctuation all impart variety and depth, both in tonal quality and geometry of space, to these richly layered poems. His poetry displays a hard-earned wisdom and insights into the human condition, the complexity of our existence, of the way human habitation works within a flawed organic form, and betrays the speaker's own disillusionment and sorrow, yet also cherishes hope in its struggle toward peace and happiness. Ralph Hamilton's work bristles with a startling candor that will not only provide clarity and understanding but also solace to the bruised heart. These are not poems to rush through. They must be entered, slowly, with sensual delight, much as a dog teases a bone in private, and with full attention. Readers should take their time with these beautiful poems, to savor and ponder, and relish the moment. They will be amply rewarded.

How to be Another
by Susan Lewis

Review by Elizabeth Nichols

Susan Lewis' *How to Be Another* lets the reader share the head-space—and the emotional landscape—of the speaker in the poems. This poetry collection suggests that the best way to know another human being is to use poetry as a vehicle to the soul. Reading Lewis' collection feels like reading the poetical equivalent of Holden Caulfield: not everything may be true, and much may be exaggerated, but there is a greater truth at hand, a revelation, waiting in the field of rye. Much like Holden's plea to the young prostitute Sunny, the speaker entreats the reader to, "...Say what you please. Just promise to listen."

From "Please Don't"

> ...In the
> boot camp of identity, the pressure is stratospheric. In the
> metropolis of my psyche, no one is major. It's a minefield in
> there, a bed of thorny roses. Someone must swim these
> waters.
> Everyone will drown.

Anxiety pins words to the page, pulling the lines taut. In the speaker's search for identity, there is a sense of standing on a precipice; of trying to "soften the landing" of an inevitable fall: "The question of thinking is a loaded gun waiting to pop the cap off / stability, which sounds like a comfortable accommodation for / jumpers or anyone likely to jump a gun." Occupying the speaker's mind—wading through a cascade of sharp wordplay and emotionally charged metaphors—is a daunting task, but one that, the speaker assures the listener, will be worthwhile:

From "Starting Gate":

> I promise to connect the dots. I promise to keep a glass eye on you. In return, you must promise something you do not want to give, such as your future. Of course, I will politely decline, but you must ignore my diffidence if we are to transcend this mortal coil & amass trophies meretricious enough to stir the neighbors, who are probably still hibernating in their plush & solipsistic canyons of doubt.

Coming to know one's self, the speaker reveals, will be painful. Even if "there's no end to questions," "no final analysis," this journey of self-discovery will be worth it to escape the hedonistic existence of a "plush" life. Like the trapped souls in Plato's allegory of the cave, "the neighbors" are content living chained to the walls of their "canyon," mistaking the shadows playing upon their rocky expanse as reality. The neighbor's existence parallels that of the speaker in the poem "Beloved," in which the speaker describes an unhealthy relationship: "I want to thank you for the cage you made. As you know, it fits my / narrow outlook to a T, better than the one I made myself. That / one, you may recall, replaced my original home." The speaker divulges that the true danger of a "solipsistic" existence is moving from one cage—one canyon—to another, never finding the truth of one's existence, one's identity.

Ultimately, the reader discovers that learning that sharing in the speaker's journey for identity was actually an exercise in coming to know himself; of recognizing the common humanity of a stranger. *How to Be Another* keeps a "glass eye" on the reader, reflecting back the reader's own image even while sharing the contents of a kindred soul through poetry.

State of the Union
by Susan Lewis

Review by Elizabeth Nichols

In Susan Lewis' collection, *State of the Union*, the distance between the poet and the reader is eradicated. Too often, the poet is put on a pedestal. He or she steps above the chatter of the masses to expound on the human condition from on high, using language that is beautiful, but dense and often too abstract for the casual reader. Lewis' collection, however, brings the poet back down to earth with confessionary, almost epistolary, poems that are in direct conversation with the reader:

From "In Which":

> To untangle this discourse, close your eyes
> & listen. To capture your own attention, release it.

> Greed is a false ally. Chance is the highest power.
> Sprinkle something tasty in the void, extend the
> licked lips of tenderness. Practice mouthing apologies
> like better prayers. Assemble your objections, then
> scatter them to the still-forgiving winds.

Lewis' lines act as directions for the reading of her poetry, but also as a way to live. Poet and reader are brought together by frank language that is all the more powerful for its cutting directness. The state of the union, the state of the inner life of poet and reader, is "...Tangled in this web of our / own mayhem, choked by too much and not enough, / looking to our slaves for affection and a workable / excuse." The reader becomes the poet's confidant, listening to the tumultuous emotions of a fellow human being overwhelmed by the world.

And in return for the reader's ear, the poet says, "I won't forget your inner life, that fine & twisted / labyrinth." The poetry in *State of the Union* is much like an inner life in and of itself; as if the reader is privy to the thoughts in both the poet's, and his own, mind. It is as if the reader is witnessing synapses firing, making connections and associations rife with meaning, but hidden from conscious thought. This is what Lewis' poetry does best.

From "Unbound by Law":

> & its antecedents, with synesthesia & justice for
> ill. Mastered, digitally + analogously, a matter of
> enfolded dimensions & simultaneity spontaneously
> irrupted, inter- of not co-, exogenously layered like
> that sexy cake you sport to shield you from the reign
> of expression—impressed as any empress, avec or
> sans portfolio.

It is clear that Lewis like to play with words, showcase her mastery of them to a meaningful, if sometimes dizzying effect. But, her wordplay is not a detrimental to understanding the poem. Words flow into words, an avalanche of meaning all strung together with playful connections. *State of the Union* allows the reader to "internalize complexity," and converse with both poet and poetry itself.

This Visit
by Susan Lewis

Review by Elizabeth Nichols

In Susan Lewis' *This Visit*, the reader is treated to a collection that, through wordplay and wit, subverts the natural order of words and senses. The twist of a sheet transforms into a suffocating trap of the mind. Eyes are transmuted into "ayes." The reader is asked if there are answers to be had in "shadows." Lewis' collection more than demonstrates that language is malleable. Like squeezing water from a rock, Lewis forces out new meanings from otherwise stagnantly defined words. And, as in the poem "Dear Random Object," sometimes Lewis gives the reader no words upon which to anchor himself:

> [dear random object] of my earnest / attention / (insert name here) / (or any notion) / until some other, / if not you / ...impostor cause / amassing *gravitas* / like heavy water / with the power / to split / & burn— / ... —& you / feel important

The reader connects with the speaker of the poem by inserting his own "name," his own "notion," into the linguistic "*gravitas*" at hand. In a reversal of roles, it is the reader that defines the subject of the poem, not the poet. Lewis' wordplay not only gives way to a subversion of language, but also of the very ideas of poet and reader.

The lines in Lewis' poems tumble on the page, spaces jutting between words, creating a sense of urgency. In the titular poem of the collection, this urgency is once again underscored by Lewis' wordplay:

From "This Visit"

> This time / which is "yours," / that face you covet, / the hurt it bleeds, / blows landing / puff with satisfaction / shamefaced as childhood, / as roundly accidental. / What is to be done / with cliff-edged blunders / howling & hollowing / your unfathomed deeps? / —As this time, / your time, / whittles you, / explodes?

In this poem about physical abuse, the reader is forced to imagine himself as the victim through the speaker's direct address of "you." Note the use of "howling & hollowing," which rhyme and are one syllable away from being homophones. By placing these two words next to each other, Lewis juxtaposes their respective meanings: a loud, baleful cry against the act of creating a cavity, an empty space. When read aloud, the effect is doubly resonant. The "howling" becomes an emptying of spirit, leaving the "fathomed depths" of the victim painfully vacuous; ready, at the slightest provocation, to lash out or collapse. The reader is forced into the mind-space of the victim, guided by Lewis' wordplay and similes into empathy.

Finally, Lewis closes *This Visit* with "Severance." The reader is told to "Pass logic, / pass the obedient word;" to transcend the usual definitions to find meaning in life. Lewis' collection allows the reader to do just that. *This Visit* into Lewis' poetry subverts language through wordplay, and redefines the role of the reader and of the poet. The reader is guided into empathizing with difficult, but important, subjects. Lewis makes poetry a synesthetic experience, creating new associations with words and the emotions that they evoke. This Visit is a tribute to the power of language and poetry to transform the reader's understanding of world.

Femme Eterna
by Lyn Lifshin

Review by Karen Bowles

It is rare to find a collection of poems that so unequivocally serves to both inspire and educate its readers, lifting them into rarefied realms steeped both in history and myth. In *Femme Eterna* from Glass Lyre Press, author Lyn Lifshin has pulled off a feat of epic engineering that "shimmers in / the hot light like / ripples on the Euphrates." Lifshin focuses her narrative magic on three colossal icons of history: Enheduanna, Scheherazade and Nefertiti. Each name touches upon elements of legend, being the earliest recorded names of women to make their mark in antiquity. *Femme Eterna* offers a chance to step into the world of literary high priestesses (Enheduanna), master storytellers (Scheherazade), and mysterious idols (Nefertiti). Readers will be enchanted as they are absorbed by each poem, witnessing the author

> carve her heart's
> words, chisel stone with
> her fierce passion, a
> world grounded in
> desire for gods and
> goddesses

Lifshin has clearly done much research to go along with her creative renderings. Unusually vivid in scope, one would be forgiven for feeling as though they had actually been transported back in time to witness these towering figures of the ancient world. Perhaps the classic women served as avatars for the author, allowing special resonance as she gave "birth to what / explodes from / her heart." Short or long in length, every verse is "free, pulsing, alive, / luminous in darkness/as Enheduanna's / poems, her words, / intense."

Each composition is birthed with care, with the poetess "carrying / the embryo of a / poem in her fingers." Honoring the sacred essences of strength and wisdom in an astute rendering of human attributes, Lifshin's stirring prose will appeal to all readers in search of "a masterpiece, vivid, / glistening." This collection sheds light upon the heritage of all writers, as Enheduanna was the first writer to inscribe her name on her work:

> a woman who couldn't
> sleep and walked out alone
> under the stars and could
> not keep what was
> pulsing inside her, dug
> her feelings into clay
> and signed her name

Lifshin is a master of "dream divination," allowing her readers to be transported into mythology while simultaneously underscoring how much like the ancestors we truly are. Readers ponder regular life dilemmas mixed with heady tastes of the celestial, facing the difficulties endured when both states crash into each other and force a choice to be made. But for those who like "stories, pungent as a / mango grove," the choice is quite easy. Do not hesitate to pick up *Femme Eterna* and watch as its words "lasso / your blood and / your dreams."

Brash Ice
by Djelloul Marbrook
Review by Elizabeth Nichols

Djelloul Marbrook's collection, *Brash Ice*, cracks the cold veneer of false identity, and reveals the true self through poetry. In *Brash Ice*, the discovery of one's true identity is not just a revelatory thawing of pretensions—not just an idyllic emergence from a dull cocoon into a world of color and easy flight. It is a painful, messy experience that leaves the individual skirting peril. The "business of being you," contends the speaker in Marbrook's opening poem, "is about handling plutonium / and is much more dangerous / than your parents said." If the discovery of one's true self is improperly handled, misguided, the result is implosive chaos. From this exploration of identity and its revelation, *Brash Ice* ultimately draws a parallel between the power of self discovery and the power of poetry.

In the titular poem of the collection, "brash ice," the speaker tells the reader that "i've said too much and said it flatly / because i thought the song pretentious / that splinters the wardrobe of the years / and shoves me out the door a naked stranger." The poem warns the reader that this collection will not sugarcoat the tumultuous experience of finding identity. Furthermore, such candied statements of self discovery distort the image of one's true self, leaving the individual "naked," exposed, but unable to recognize the skin that hid beneath the "wardrobe." This cognitive dissonance leaves the individual in a state of anxious crisis, "dying" of "secret nakedness."

But, *Brash Ice* will not leave the reader in such a state. Instead, when one's true self is discovered, crisis will be averted by accepting the ugly, as well as the beautiful, parts of the soul. It is the gray matter, not the veneer of idol-white or demon-black, that makes a person most recognizably human. In the poem "demons take your seats," the speaker addresses the demons that live his soul:

> it was urgent that i speak,
> demons, take your seats,
> so that the inevitable
> might be postponed
> until this distant day
> when shutting up would seem
> a bargain and i would wink
> at your patient horrors
> knowing i am one of you.

By addressing the demons—the sins—that live in his soul, the speaker acknowledges every part of his self. Instead of living in willful ignorance of his inner demons, winking at their horrors, the speaker chooses to embrace the darkest parts of himself in order to discover the truth. The speaker escapes from a self-inflicted purgatory by recognizing that demons are inevitable, and self actualization lies with the acceptance or denial of those inner demons. The journey of self-discovery will involve conversing with demons, and garnering an understanding of what it means to be fully human.

Finally, Marbrook's poem, "do not ask" draws a parallel between self-discovery and the power of poetry. Poetry is both a vehicle that can be used to uncover one's true identity, and a result of the search for identity. In "do not ask," the speaker directly addresses the reader, offering education and revelation:

> i will bring to you everyone you need
> i will bring you to everyone you need
> if only you do not ask me who i am.
> i will teach you to swim in the eye of desire
> and not drown, i will teach you to reemerge
> as the thousands you have been before
> and then to bind sheaves of comets
> to light the corridors of my mind.

It is not a nameless speaker that addresses the reader, but poetry personified. Poetry entreats thereader not to ask "who i am," because poetry has the power to take on all identities: contain multitudes. Poetry does not only stand for the poet who composed its lines and stanzas, but for all the readers that derive meaning from it. By reading poetry, the reader "reemerges / as the thousands" she has "been before," because poetry has the power to describe the human condition. Marbrook's *Brash Ice* "lights the corridors" of the reader's mind, revealing the human as a being that is both demon and angel, pained and exultant. *Brash Ice* takes the raw, icy material of false identity and sculpts it into a brilliantly clear, and endlessly faceted figure that refracts countless prismatic images of the human.

The Lifeline Trembles
by Mary Kay Rummel

Review by Elizabeth Nichols

Mary Kay Rummel's *The Lifeline Trembles* plucks at the threads of life like the greek goddesses of fate. In this collection, Rummel weaves poems into a grand tapestry of life, sewing the together the sinews of the human condition with evocative language. While the greek goddesses of fate gather up threads of life, Rummel—as a poet—gathers up words and spins them into poetry. By extension, the lines of Rummel's poems can be seen as a manifestation of the threads of fate, as both poetry and the threads of fate contain the essence of humanity. Rummel's poetry leaves the reader "weaving, forever weaving / into and out of this world," marveling at the interwoven threads of life.

For the speaker in Rummel's poems, the act of writing poetry involves giving away a piece of herself: of revealing irrepressible desires. In "The Unicorn Tapestries," poetry becomes a sensory experience. Like a cup overflowing, the speaker cannot help but let the roiling sea of her senses spill onto the "map" of the page:

> It's time to give you away now
> my chest full of words,
> tongue-flood, my one desire—
> lark, scent of cardamom,
> lilac moon.

> Words are the colors I swim.
> My heart the cartographer
> charts the water....

The poem also comments on the mindset of the poet in the process of writing poetry. The poet is likened to a cartographer, but instead of charting the size of oceans, she instead reveals the depths of her own inner world. In addition, "The Unicorn Tapestries" shows what the collection as a whole will do for the reader. Namely, that the poet will share her vision of the world, and of herself. The poem "Ars Poetica" also speaks to the poet's feelings about her own writing: a poem waits for me to see it / the way Monet's last painting / his exact pink and red primroses / waited for his uncurtained vision." *The Lifeline Trembles* unveils the world through a poet's eyes. The reader is drawn to "the man behind the curtain—" to the poet that does "not want to die without writing" her "watery unwritten universe."

The world as revealed to the reader by the poet is one of effervescent beauty, its wonders glistening like richly hued gems. In "A Belane Tapestry," the reader is dazzled by the beauty of the world, left disoriented by its majesty:

> Shine is all you see.
> It glitters, seduces
> in this ordered fading world.
> Suddenly you tremble,
> a lone poplar welcoming
> its finches home.

Here, the poet captures the dual meaning of the word "awesome," which is not only to inspire admiration, but also fear. The poem elicits comparisons to the transcendentalists, like Thoreau, who marveled at nature with a fearful spiritual revelry. The poem's last stanza harkens back to the collection's title, and signals that it is not just the poet whose inner life is revealed, but the reader's, as well: "you tremble" at what poetry has brought home to roost.

But, there is more to *The Lifeline Trembles* than revelation. In "Palimpsest," the reader begins with answers, which become "bruised trees," "clouds," or physical sensations. A palimpsest is something reused or altered, but still bearing visible traces of its earlier form. In the poem, everything is interconnected, flowing into one thing and then another to create new meaning:

From "Palimpsest"

> If by words you mean answers
> where the moon tilts on its side
> like a burning blade
>
> If by answer you mean bruised trees,
> clouds, lights of a far-off city, or the way
> your finger slides into my closed fist
>
> trembling the lifeline, the way
> your palms resurrect my breasts.

"Palimpsest" explores the deep connections that seemingly unconnected things have with one another. The reader begins with a bird's eye view of images—the "moon," the "bruised trees—" and is gently brought down to a scene of intimacy. All the sensory input of the world is hyper-focused onto an intimate bonding moment. That a lead-in of intangible connections turns into a tangible one is not an accident. The speaker in the poem is the palimpsest: still herself, and yet forever altered by this encounter. By extension, the reader is also a palimpsest: still himself, but forever altered by poetry.

The Lifeline Trembles plays upon the pulse of life like a bow makes violin strings sing, creating the music of the world, the music of ourselves. In Rummel's collection, "words sprout" from the "heart like mallow," sharing a complex inner life with the reader. *The Lifeline Trembles* allows the reader to see the world through the poet's eyes, lifting a veil from the world like the sun banishing fog. Beauty is revealed, and the reader is left dazzled by the awesome revelations that poetry has wrought. Rummel's mastery of the senses, of language, and poetry ensures that, like the speaker in "Burnt Dress," the reader will keep returning to *The Lifeline Trembles*—Rummel's "words" like "stones" he "keep[s] fingering."

The Greenhouse
by Lisa Gluskin Stonestreet

Review by Elizabeth Nichols

Do not expect to find mere posies in Lisa Gluskin Stonestreet's *The Greenhouse*. This chapbook is a hotbed of lyrical language, of words that bring the joys and struggles of motherhood to life. Stonestreet's poetry flows on the page, her words like watercolors over-saturating, and warping the page until it has a new color and form. Stonestreet's poetic exploration of motherhood is reminiscent of Mary Cassat's famous paintings of mothers and their children. Indeed, the tenderness evoked in Cassat's work, such as the well-known oil painting *The Child's Bath*, seems to have been transmuted into lines of poetry from the painter's brushstrokes. Stonestreet's poems resonate with warmth and a precious delicateness, feelings often associated with motherhood. But, in this greenhouse, there is more growing than just glowing recommendations of child-rearing. In *The Greenhouse*, mother and child are complex, interconnected beings — each stunningly imperfect, and fallible, in their humanity.

In the poem "Like That," the speaker conveys a sense of shared existence with her child. During pregnancy, the mother shares her body with the child, but after birth this physical connection is severed. The speaker, the mother, grapples with the child's absence from her body:

From "Like That"
>
> The first time
>
>   I leaned over and swept the tip of my smallest fingernail down into
>
> the whorl of your ear (*bigger than your elbow*), and you yelped
>
> in violation:
>
>   forgive me
>
> it is not longer my ear
>
>   (little boat, little shell I carved)....

Stonestreet's lines spread out, leaving space between images and ideas to create new resonance and meaning. Here, the physical separation of mother from her child is expressed with the spaces between the lines. The symbiotic relationship between mother and child is over, but the speaker in the poem still feels, "...everything slipping, permeable, you/ me / the least of it: / day/night / inside/outside / body/body...." The greenhouse is a metaphor for the mother's womb, and "Like That" is one Stonestreet's poems that addresses what happens when the life growing inside the greenhouse abruptly leaves.

This emphasis on permeability also lends itself to another one of this collections themes: the flowing, cyclical nature of time. In "Flowers, Doggies, the Moon," the rhythms of life are played out like ocean tides, flowing in and out with routine and memory. "The present" nudges "at the shore" of the speaker's consciousness, pulling her back from contemplations of the past. But, still, the speaker cannot help getting "the lines tangled:"

From "Flowers, Doggies, the Moon"

> Even out there, the lines get tangled. Especially out there. Each hull / throwing out a line to the next, a web, a path back to not- / here not-now, back on the shore / of the phone call, the gas bill, the poem and how it should end, the need / to show up tethered to the tug on the other end: and it's so easy to see myself hopping from / one to the next, to link them like metaphor until all the clocks line up on either side and the / kitchen and the desk are sparkling empty, arrayed....

The images of the "phone call," the "gas bill," the "poem", and the "clocks" all jumble together in a carefully crafted expression of chaos. And, yet, anchoring the chaotic activity in the poem is the sense that there is a greater purpose in the madness at hand. "One" thing "to the next" is linked, interconnected, as an expression of life, of flowing time. It is easy to imagine the stay-at-home parent lost in the web of this chaos, but at the same time driven to the culmination of it all in the raising of a child.

Finally, in one of Stonestreet's strongest poems, the symbiotic relationship between mother and child, and the expression of cyclical time, are combined. In "Chimera," the note preceding the poem explains that, "Microchimerism is the persistent presence of a few genetically distinct cells in an organism ... cells containing the male Y chromosome were found circulating in the blood of women after pregnancy." In Greek mythology, the chimera was a creature made up of many creatures: the lion, the snake, and the goat. Here, with the male Y chromosome cells still circulating in the mother's blood, the female body is imagined as a chimera: a being made up of more than one human.

From "Chimera"

> I want them out. I want
> to be myself, my self
> again. My own untethered,
>
> young, untried."
>
> ...The crucible

>   does not ask
>   for want. Is. Tied in,
>   shot through. Fired.

Although the child is now birthed from the mother's body, the speaker still experiences a loss of her former self. She still feels *other*. She is torn between wanting to be what she was before, and what she is now. In addition, the speaker likens her body to a crucible, which is a container that can withstand very high temperatures metal production, and lab processes. In this case, the woman's body has withstood the intense creation of another human being. The speaker's body is irreparably changed. Unlike the sentiment expressed in "Like That," here the speaker feels no sense of separation from her child and, in fact, will always carry a part of her child with her. In essence, there is a part of the speaker's body that will always connect her to the past: that will bring her back to gestation of her child, and to her memories.

Stonestreet's *Greenhouse* leaves the reader with more than just an aura of maternal warmth. Instead, this collection revels in the complexity of motherhood, and shares the interconnected world of mother and child. In Stonestreet's *Greenhouse*, poetry is birthed from one of the most beautiful and potent of human experiences, creating expressions of 'mother' and 'child' that are at once achingly familiar and refreshingly new.

I Ate the Cosmos for Breakfast
by Melissa Studdard

Review by Elizabeth Nichols

Melissa Studdard's collection *I Ate the Cosmos for Breakfast* contains many dimensions of human life. While spirituality is what thematically connects the poems in the collection, it is the interconnected nature of human life that takes center stage in *I Ate the Cosmos for Breakfast*. Like a golden halo of flames, the images in Studdard's poetry emit an ebullient glow, even if those images depict mundane moments in human life—like eating breakfast. In the end, Studdard's poetry demonstrates that interconnectedness is at the heart of spirituality, and the recognition of that revelation is not so much a matter of religion as it is a matter of being wholly human.

The collection opens with a "Creation Myth." It is fitting that the first poem in *I Ate the Cosmos for Breakfast* is a creation myth, because it sets the tone for the rest of the collection. At the same time, it tells the reader something about the kind of spirituality at work in Studdard's poems. Namely, that this is a spirituality rooted in love, in interconnectedness, and and poetry.

From "Creation Myth"

> So there God lay, with her legs splayed,
> birthing this screaming world....

> It wasn't just pebbles and boulders
> and patches of sky, but the soul of sunlight,
> the spirit of moon.
>
> ...
>
> and she glowed—like a woman
> in love with her own making, infatuated
>
> with all corners of the blemished universe,
> smitten with every imperfect thing:
>
> splotchy, red-faced & wailing—
> flawless in her omniscient eyes.

Here, God is notably female and not male. The creation of the universe is imagined not as an omnipotent wave of a hand, but as a physical birthing. With a physical as well as emotional connection to her creations, God is a much more empathetic figure. God becomes nurturing—maternally aglow with love for her creations. In this sense, God is aligned more closely with nature, which is often described with similar maternal overtones. Critically, the reader is made to understand that love is the lifeblood of spirituality: a love that, despite its imperfection, its "splotchy, red-face," drives humanity to reach for deep connections and meaning in life.

In the titular poem of the collection, "I Ate the Cosmos for Breakfast," a mundane moment in human life is set on a grand scale. On the surface, it is a poem about thanksgiving—about recognizing the work of many that goes into a meal for one. But, more than that, it is a poem about the the invisible ties that bind people together. Studdard's charged language and striking images make the act of eating breakfast a meditative exercise in which to consume food is also to partake in the richness of human life. In "I Ate the Cosmos for Breakfast," the speaker cracks open an egg, and undergoes a humanist communion:

> It looked like a pancake,
> but it was creation flattened out—
> the fist of God on a head of wheat,

>   milk, the first unborn child of an unsuspecting
>   chicken—all beaten to batter
>   and drizzled into a pan.
>   I brewed some tea and closed my eyes
>   while I ate the sun, the air, the rain,
>   photosynthesis on a plate.
>   I ate the time it took that chicken
>   to bear and lay her egg
>   and the energy a cow takes
>   to lactate a cup of milk.
>   I thought of the farmers, the truck drivers,
>   the grocers, the people
>   who made the bag that stored the wheat,
>   and my labor over the stove seemed short,
>   and the pancake tasted good,
>   and I was thankful.

Here, interconnectedness is clearly demonstrated. The breaking of the speaker's fast is "flattened out," revealing every ingredient, every hand at work, in the making of the meal. The external forces at work in the creation of the breakfast are teased out, and shown to directly impact the speaker. There is also a transference of energy from the beings that create the food, like "the chicken" and the "cow," to the consumer of the food. The "farmers" and the "truck drivers" also add manual energy into the mix by processing the food. By extension, as the reader absorbs the meaning of the poem—just as surely as the speaker absorbs the nutrients of her breakfast—the reader is uplifted by a pure expression of the human spirit: poetry itself.

Studdard's collection also incorporates references to art and influential poets of the past, such as Johannes Vermeer's painting *A Young Woman with a Water Jug*, and the work of the modernist poet Charles Baudelaire. Specifically, the poem "For Baudelaire" uses the work of said modernist poet to comment on the cyclical nature of life:

>   In the woods you found a carcass with maggots in its chest,
>   with waterfalls in its eyes, with the buzz of life still
>
>   hovering around its skull, and in commemoration, you grabbed
>   your sweetheart's hand, with your left, and on your right, you

snatched the clasped hand of the world and said: Look here, how
we build skyscrapers in the cavity of death's groin, how we

paint lilacs on its ribs. We will drive motor cars over its
bones and laugh in the waning perfume of midnight, and, my love,

I will write you a poem, a tribute to your beautiful decay,
to your rotting thighs, to the death you will birth with sex

because, truly, this is beauty— this festering carcass in the woods,
this putrid nag, truth. And in it, you will live forever."

In death, the body becomes a symbol. Despite the fact that the body itself is dead, it turns into a host for other life forms, like "maggots." The speaker finds beauty in the image of the deceased because life springs from death. From tragedy and loss, man "builds skyscrapers." To recognize "beautiful decay" is to live life laughing "in the waning perfume of night," knowing that death is the inevitable end. Here, death is the wellspring of poetry. And, as other poets have observed, poetry is the means by which man will live forever. Poetry has a vital role to play in the cycle of life and death: it explores the meaning of existence, and breaks free of the cycle itself.

Studdard's spirituality of life, interconnectedness, and poetry has come full circle. *I Ate the Cosmos for Breakfast* delves deep into the physical, emotional, and spiritual aspects of human life and, in doing so, leaves the reader with a mouth and heart full of the richness and beauty of existence. Studdard's imagery lingers on the tongue, sweetening with every taste of her metaphors and creative language. With Studdard's collection, the reader is transported to "the other realm, the one beneath the skin, beneath / the bone and marrow and veiny streams of blood, where gods / await" him "like lovers," "like cracked / and forgotten mirrors, reflecting the singular route home." *I Ate the Cosmos for Breakfast* fleshes out the connections between human beings, between the mundane and the spiritual and, ultimately, it is all poetry.

Blood Flower
by Pamela Uschuk

Review by Ami Kaye & Linda Kim

The poems in *Blood Flower* by Pamela Uschuk are deftly woven meditations of intricate beauty and strength, delicate as spider silk. They shimmer with nuanced mystery and an alluring wildness. Riotous color spills from each poem along with lyrics of clarity and subtle meaning. They render memory, raw and primal, as haunting displays of human motivation. Uschuk's charged language and its tumultuous music hits the reader with the ferocity of an emotional hurricane, as in poems like the sumptuous "Iron and Lace,"

>   before Bach seizes her strings
> squeezes air from the hall, quickening us
> to believe in the wet reams of blossoms, sweet
> agony of tulips slashed by rain
> or cliff swallows taking needles of twilight
> into their open beaks, stitching
> sky's ripped hem.

Blood Flower addresses various lives built from blood and strife against the sharply contrasted backdrops of Russia and America. Violence and peace, earth and humanity, and wilderness and urbanization are also juxtaposed. Uschuk is an ecofeminist, an activist, and a wilderness advocate; this informs her poetry. Mother Earth is both a character and a setting. Fresh details anchor the narrative thrust of the poems, layered with depth and discovery. Warmth emanates from the comfort of familiar, from the bones of family, "brewing borscht thick as mating musk/ to heal all grief" (p. 13), and the deep knowledge of one's heritage, "It is the Russian in me that charges out/ in my dark velvet skirts" (p. 27). The elements are also an integral part of Uschuk's vast repertoire (p. 29),

> Some music is wind, some
> cherry wood flames fed
> by blond sticks of birch
> crackling a St. Petersburg stove.

There is a deep love of Russia's rich culture and history, as well as family. This awareness of localism is ever present, further emphasizing the chasm between her Russian and American point of views. Physical displacement from the wilder homeland of Russia to the tamed and dominated landscapes of America reveals a discontent with society, the exploitation of the earth, and the legacy of violence. "Red Menace" (p. 5) clearly highlights Uschuk's skill at transforming abstract concepts into vital imagery, "They knew. / In their very simplest syllables, / they knew— / Jones, Pierce, Drew— / Russian rides roughshod, / a Tartar horseman across / the tongue, dances / tranced as the bear / Siberian shamans become. / Too many consonants befuddle, / breed fear in the ear / of the English-speaking host" (p. 5). This poem, one of the earliest in the book, establishes the divide Uschuk keenly felt throughout her childhood as she grew up in America as an outsider. Uschuk's awareness of and respect toward Russian history, culture, and identity shows in the twining images of Russian steppes and horsemen, animals, and paganism. However, she contrasts it starkly with American linguistics and aesthetics, creating further conflicts within her Russian-American upbringing, a trope of immigrant narratives.

Chernobyl, one of the world's most catastrophic instances of human neglect and environmental exploitation, transforms into a pristine place of healing for victimized animals who can only thrive in isolation. Isolation is a key component of Uschuk's admiration of Russian wilderness. Destruction begets restoration just as winter will always transition to spring. This dynamic of winter is entrenched Russian psychology and identity. Although winter is always harsh, further cementing the Russian world view, Uschuk shows a gentler and more nurturing side of it.

"Genesis Revisited: The Chernobyl Buffalo" (p. 38) is a study in nature reclamation. Is Eden an impossible ideal in such a violent, caustic world? But she appropriates the typical dystopic narrative of Chernobyl's destruction and instead turns it into a story of triumph for nature. "Against toxic apartment walls, crumbling schools, / an echoing hospital, wolves curl / against howling winter snows. Come spring, buffalo / graze at ease between sprouting deciduous trees / that were once shopping malls" (page 38). Buffalos have returned. Genesis is restored. Nature is a story of renewal and growth in the absence of invading humanity. Violence upon the earth engenders extinction of animals, which can only foreshadow the extinction of humans through their own self-destructive tendencies.

In "The Trick" (p. 45) technology further removes humanity from the earth, which is ultimately to our detriment. The more advanced technology becomes, the better humans get at killing each other. The earth is constantly wounded like soldiers are constantly killed. Uschuk is troubled by how television reinforces the distance between home and faraway wars like the Vietnam War. Detachment and apathy are dangerous attitudes for civilians to have because with them there can be no urgency to condemn war. The reality contained within a television screen can't possibly do justice to the true horrors of war. "TV bombarded us with the severed / limbs of charred children, / napalm-snuffed villages, a whole / country disemboweled every night at dinner. / You wrote me that you stood / on top of an ambulance while mortars / tore wounds in the green earth, / and you couldn't stop anyone's screams. / So far from answers, I mailed cookies, / chocolate and poems, but / I couldn't send you snow banks / or the way to come home" (p. 45).

"Ruined Honey" (p. 53) humanizes the anonymous victims of war while highlighting the wasteful senselessness of it all and the tragedy of loss. "Her back, machine-gunned, / stains with orange-sized wounds. / She jerks in yellow dust. / What is not seen is that / those slugs draw a skewer of blood / between mother and child. / What is not seen is / that morning, the woman heard her baby / laugh, dipped her forefinger in honey, then / rubbed her child's lips / to make laughter come again" (p. 53). This is one of many poems that illustrates a mother's point of view. Uschuk returns again and again to the portrait of the young mother in the context of war so as to create a stark, gut-punching pictures. As a poet, she is taken with this archetype of innocence lost because it perfectly ties in with her ecofeminism and how nature is continually harmed through the destructive force of man.

The grief in "Veterans Day" (p. 69), is palpable when the speaker says, "My lost soldiers / are ash. Father. Brother. Husband. Their stories circle / like crows, cawing machine gun rounds / or pop like the single-shot from a 45 that bloodied / my father's tent when his friend / blasted his teeth into his brain, writing / his own discharge papers from war" (p. 69). Uschuk is aware of this circular narrative of war, a pattern of tragedy that continually repeats to no one's benefit, especially those left behind. The crows are harbingers of death circling over the corpses on the battlefield, with their harsh dissonant caws aurally conflating with the blasts of gunpowder. In Section 2 overt images of violence are common. It is telling that this stanza ends with the father's friend preferring suicide over a combat death, showing the lengths soldiers will go to escape both the physical trap of endless violence, as well as the spiritual death of their souls. PTSD is a common feature in Uschuk's imaginings of soldiers. As the book progresses, there is a tonal shift from a brittle bitterness to a more sorrowful and contemplative tone, which focuses more on grief and the question of the heart's resilience.

"Fire Song" (p. 83) is one of the book's later poems that cements the thematic development of the book. "I am a nun in my garden, dreaming rain / to pound into earth's cracked and neglected hips. / I feel sorry for the trees, spray piñon and juniper / needles so dry they snap when I squeeze them. / I read that, in Sudan, where women are stoned / to death, drought widens its clipped grin" (p. 83). The suggestion of violence in the snap of dry needles give way to an overt image of political violence. Uschuk explores the Mother Earth archetype, with motherhood as a setting for her political concerns. Nature's divine cycle restores and renews, while violence is a disruptive cycle of humanity that can only destroy. This is evident in the way Uschuk addresses violence, political warfare, feminism, and the treatment of the environment. *Blood Flower* is a wholly appropriate title, as a blood-stained flower is a central argument to the book.

These poems are ecstatic explorations, intersections of space and memory, where literary traditions are reinvented with a strong lyric force, but they are far more, in their intrinsic and profound wisdom. The poems in *Blood Flower* are lucid, sensuous and compelling, fed by the heat of Uschuk's language. The dazzling, incandescent quality of her writing gives life to the richly textured lines in this book, "red velvet vulva of roses/hum in the humming light/as this music lifts only to drop us/shattering like crystal glasses/thrown onto the stone cold hearth of alone" (p. 31). In *Blood Flower*, where "Each note's small coal singes our wrists" (p.30), Pamela Uschuk taps into the source of song itself,

> It is as if a flock of hummingbirds
> has swarmed into the concert hall, begging
> forgiveness from the mouths of trumpet flowers
> whose nectar they drink to live. (p. 33)

Publication Credits

Lois P. Jones "How She Paints Herself"
First appeared in *Awakenings*

"Unmarked Grave"
First appeared in *American Poetry Journal*

"The Scent of Ariel"
First appeared in *Tiferet*

Allison Joseph "Extraction"
First appeared in Voice: Poems (Mayapple Press, 2009)

"Little Epiphanies"
First appeared in Valparaiso Poetry Review

"Makeover: Esmerelda's House of Beauty"
First appeared in Mezzo Cammin (Vol.3, Issue 1)

"On Being Told I Don't Speak Like a Black Person"
First appeared in Carnegie Mellon University Press

"Sex: A Lesson"
First appeared on Ducts.org (Issue 34, Winter 2015)

"Sonnet for a Good Mood"
First appeared on WomenMade.org; republished in *Little Epiphanies* (Imaginary Friend Press, 2015)

"Sundown Ghazal"
First appeared in Heart Online (Dec. 1, 2013); republished in *Little Epiphanies* (Imaginary Friend Press, 2015)

"Why Poets Should Dance"
First appeared in *Soul Train* (Carnegie Mellon University Press, 1997)

Contributor Notes

Jim Pascual Agustin writes and translates poetry in Filipino and English. He grew up in the Philippines during the Marcos dictatorship. He moved to Cape Town, South Africa in 1994. Some of the publications where his work has appeared are *New Coin* (SA), *Rhino Poetry* (USA), and *Modern Poetry in Translation* (UK). His books of poetry before leaving Manila are *Beneath an Angry Star* (Anvil, 1992) and *Salimbayan* (Publikasyong Sipat, 1994). Two books were simultaneously released by the University of Santo Tomas Publishing House in Manila in 2011: *Baha-bahagdang Karupukan* (poems in Filipino) and *Alien to Any Skin* (poems in English). The same publisher released two new collections in 2013: *Kalmot ng Pusa sa Tagiliran* (poems in Filipino) and *Sound Before Water* (poems in English). Forthcoming in 2015 is a collection of short stories in Filipino, *Sanga sa Basang Lupa*, and a new poetry collection, *A Thousand Eyes*. His blog is www.matangmanok.wordpress.com.

R. Steve Benson studied poetry with the late poet James Hearst – friend of Paul Engle, Robert Frost & Carl Sandburg – at the University of Northern Iowa. Married, he's a retired art teacher with three grown children. He lives in Mt. Vernon, Iowa. His poems have been published in many literary journals across America.

George Bishop's work has appeared in *Kentucky Review* & *Flare*. Forthcoming work will be featured in *Carolina Quarterly* & *Toadlilly Press*. *Toadlilly Press* will include his latest chapbook, *Short Lives & Solitudes*. Bishop won the 2013 Peter Meinke Prize at YellowJacket Press for his sixth chapbook *Following Myself Home*. He attended Rutgers University and lives and writes in Saint Cloud, Florida.

Karina Borowicz is the author of two poetry collections, *Proof* (Codhill Press, 2014) and *The Bees Are Waiting* (Marick Press, 2012), which won the Eric Hoffer Award for Poetry and was named a Must-Read by the Massachusetts Center for the Book. Her poems have appeared widely in literary journals and have been featured on Garrison Keillor's *A Writer's Almanac* and in Ted Kooser's *American Life in Poetry* series.

Karen Bowles is the founder, publisher and editor of *Luciole Press* (www.luciolepress.com). She gained the nickname "Firefly" from a friend for her enduring love of the glowbugs in the South; "Luciole" means firefly in French. She graduated from San Francisco State University with a B.A. in

Literature, and loves photography, reading, writing, theatre, and painting. After spending many years moving around, this military brat has laid down roots in Northern California, where you can find her gazing at stars and arguing with the bossy blue jay in her backyard. (www.facebook.com/BowlesKaren)

Julie Brooks Barbour is the author of *Small Chimes* (2014) and two chapbooks: *Earth Lust* (forthcoming in 2014) and *Come To Me and Drink* (2012). Her poems have appeared in *Waccamaw, diode, storySouth, Prime Number Magazine, The Rumpus, The Lindenwood Review, Midwestern Gothic, Rose Red Review, Blue Lyra Review,* and *Verse Daily*. She is co-editor of the journal *Border Crossing* and an Associate Poetry Editor at *Connotation Press: An Online Artifact*. She is an Assistant Professor of English at Lake Superior State University. Visit her online at juliebrooksbarbour.com.

Jody Burke-Kaiser was born barefoot in the Appalachian foothills to a family long steeped in storytelling and sarcasm. When she was 22 she cut her hair, giving the long red braid to an undeserving boy and set off to pursue her big city dreams. She earned a Masters degree in English from Boston College and met the love of her life on the subway platform at Harvard Square. After teaching freshman composition to hungover hockey players at 8AM on Monday morning for one year, she decided maybe she was getting to them too late to really make a difference in their lives. So, she went back to school and became a nurse-midwife. Because when it comes to talking with young folk about the joys and risks of poetry, it is best to start early. Her work has previously appeared in *The Louisville Review, Medicinal Purposes, Exact Change Only, After Hours,* and *RHINO*. She lives in Lincoln Park with the boy from the subway and their three half feral sons.

Jeremy Cantor's first poetry collection, *Wisteria from Seed*, was released this year by Alabaster Leaves Publishing, an imprint of Kelsay Books. A booklet of his haiku and senryu, *The Owl at Sunset*, was just released by Leaf Press of Vancouver, Canada. His poem "The Nietzsche Contrapositive," won the *Grey Sparrow Journal's* 2014 Flash & Poetry Competition. His work has appeared in *The Naugatuck River Review, Glassworks, The Bicycle Review, Forge, Convergence, Poetalk* and other journals.

Jeremy began writing poetry shortly before retiring from a career in laboratory chemistry. He has cleared tables and washed dishes, made and tested detergents, pharmaceuticals and engine oil additives, driven a forklift, spent time in a full-body acid-proof hazmat suit, tried to keep his fingers working in a walk-in freezer at -40°F and worked behind radiation shielding. He prefers writing.

Patricia Caspers is the founding editor of *West Trestle Review* and poetry editor of *Prick of the Spindle*. Her poems have appeared most recently in *Quiddity*, *PANK*, and *Fjord's*, and she has work forthcoming from *r.k.v.r.y* and *Superstition Review*. Her full-length collection, *In the Belly of the Albatross*, is available from Glass Lyre Press.

Karen Craigo is the author of two chapbooks, most recently *Someone Could Build Something Here* (Winged City, 2013). She lives and works in Springfield, Missouri, and is the author of a daily blog, *Better View of the Moon* (http://betterviewofthemoon.blogspot.com).

Rachel Dacus is the author of *Gods of Water and Air*, a collection of poetry, prose, and drama. Her poetry collections are *Earth Lessons* and *Femme au Chapeau*, and the spoken word CD *A God You Can Dance*. Her writing has appeared in *The Atlanta Review, Drunken Boat, Pirene's Fountain, Prairie Schooner, The Valparaiso Poetry Review*, and many other journals and anthologies. She's currently at work on a time travel novel involving the great Baroque sculptor, Gian Lorenzo Bernini. She lives in Walnut Creek, California and raises funds for nonprofit organizations.

Dennis Etzel Jr. lives with Carrie and the boys in Topeka, Kansas where he teaches English at Washburn University. His chapbook *The Sum of Two Mothers* was released by ELJ Publications in 2013. His work has appeared in *Denver Quarterly, Indiana Review, BlazeVOX, Fact-Simile, 1913: a journal of poetic forms, 3:AM, DIAGRAM*, and others. He is a TALK Scholar and Speaker for the Kansas Humanities Council, and volunteers at the YWCA of Topeka and Midland Hospice.

Patricia Fargnoli, the NH Poet Laureate from 2006-2009, has published 7 collections of poetry. Her latest book is *WINTER*, Hobblebush Books, 2013. Her books have won several awards: The May Swenson Book Award, the Sheila Mooton Book Award, The NH Literary Award.

She was a MacDowell Fellow and has published widely; most recently in *Barrow Street, Valparaiso Poetry Review, Crab Creek Review, Alaska Quarterly* and *Rattle*.

Ruth Foley lives in Massachusetts, where she teaches English for Wheaton College. Her work appears in numerous web and print journals, including *The Bellingham Review, The Louisville Review, Redheaded Stepchild,* and *Umbrella*. Her chapbook *Dear Turquoise* is available from Dancing Girl Press. She serves as Managing Editor for *Cider Press Review*.

Trina Gaynon's poems appear in the anthologies *Saint Peter's B-list: Contemporary Poems Inspired by the Saints, Obsession: Sestinas for the 21st Century, A Ritual to Read Together: Poems in Conversation with William Stafford, Phoenix Rising from the Ashes: Anthology of Sonnets of the Early Third Millennium, Bombshells* and *Knocking at the Door*, as well as numerous journals including *Natural Bridge, Reed* and the final issue of *Runes*. Her chapbook *An Alphabet of Romance* is available from Finishing Line Press.

Gail Goepfert's poetry has appeared in anthologies, print and online journals including *Avocet, After Hours, Caesura, Florida English, Uproot Magazine, Homeopathy Today, Jet Fuel Review, Examined Life Journal,* and *Ardor* among others. Currently, she serves as associate editor for *RHINO* magazine, Evanston, Illinois. She was nominated for a Pushcart Prize in 2013. Traveling is a passion; she often finds poetry a way to translate the world she sees through the camera lens.

Hedy Habra is the author of a poetry collection, *Tea in Heliopolis*, winner of the 2014 USA Best Book Awards and finalist for the 2014 International Book Award; a story collection, *Flying Carpets*, winner of the 2013 Arab American National Book Award's Honorable Mention and finalist for the USA Best Book Awards and the 2014 Eric Hoffer Book Award. She is a recipient of the 2012 Nazim Hikmet Poetry Award. Her multilingual work has appeared in more than forty journals and fifteen anthologies, including *Connotation Press, Poetic Diversity, Verse Daily, Blue Fifth Review, Nimrod, New York Quarterly, Drunken Boat, Diode, The Bitter Oleander, Cider Press Review,* and *Poet Lore*. Her website is HedyHabra.com

Taylor Haman is currently an undergraduate at Carroll University. Her work has appeared in *Century Magazine, Red Cedar,* and *Polaris*. She is the editor and co-founder at *Portage: A review of upper Midwestern writing, art, and culture*. She also co-edits *Century Magazine*.

A.J. Huffman has published seven solo chapbooks and one joint chapbook through various small presses. Her eighth solo chapbook, *Drippings from a Painted Mind*, won the 2013 Two Wolves Chapbook Contest. She also has a full-length poetry collection scheduled for release in June 2005, titled, *A Few Bullets Short of Home* (mgv2>publishing). She is a Pushcart Prize nominee, and her poetry, fiction, and haiku have appeared in hundreds of national and international journals, including *Labletter, The James Dickey Review, Bone Orchard, EgoPHobia, Kritya,* and *Offerta Speciale*, in which her work appeared in both English and Italian translations. She is also the founding editor of Kind of a Hurricane Press. www.kindofahurricanepress.com

Lois P. Jones has work published or forthcoming in *Pirene's Fountain* and *Cultural Weekly*, as well as anthologies including *The Poet's Quest for God* (Eyewear Publishing), *Wide Awake: Poetry of Los Angeles and Beyond* (The Pacific Coast Poetry Series), *30 Days* (Tupelo Press) and *Good-Bye Mexico* (Texas Review Press). Some publications include *Narrative, Tupelo Quarterly, The Warwick Review, Tiferet* and *Cider Press Review*. She is the winner of the 2012 Tiferet Poetry Prize and the 2012 Liakoura Prize. In 2015, her poem was long-listed in The Poetry Society's National Poetry Competition. She is Poetry Editor of *Kyoto Journal*, host of KPFK's *Poets Café*, co-host of Moonday Poetry and interviewer at *American Micro Reviews and Interviews*.

Allison Joseph lives, writes, teaches and runs in Carbondale, Illinois, where she is on the faculty of Southern Illinois University. Her latest books are *My Father's Kites* (Steel Toe Press) and *Trace Particles* (Backbone Press). She recently received the Paladin Award from Rhino Magazine.

Alan S. Kleiman is the author of *GRAND SLAM*, a collection of poems published by Crisis Chronicles Press. His poetry appears in numerous magazines and journals including *Yareah, Verse Wisconsin, The Criterion, Right Hand Pointing, Camel Saloon, Stone Path Review,* and *AfricanHadithi*. His poems are in anthologies published by Fine Line Press and Red Ochre Press and have been translated into Spanish, Russian, Polish, Norwegian, Danish and Ukrainian. He appeared at the Virginia Museum of Fine Arts as a featured poet in the performing arts series. Alan lives in New York City and works as an attorney when not writing poems.

Laurie Kolp is an award-winning poet with more than three dozen publications worldwide, including the 2015 *Poet's Market*, *Blue Fifth Review*, *Referential*, *Pirene's Fountain*, *contemporary haibun online (cho)* and Diane Lockward's *The Crafty Poet*. Laurie's first full-length poetry collection, *Upon the Blue Couch* (Winter Goose Publishing), is available on Amazon. Learn more about Laurie here: http://lauriekolp.com.

Richard Krawiec's third book of poems, *Women Who Loved me Despite*, will be out in March, 2015. His second book of poems, *She Hands me the Razor*, was one of 17 finalists for a SIBA Award. His work appears in dozens of literary magazines, including *New Orleans Review*, *Drunken Boat*, *Shenandoah*, *sou'wester*, *Dublin Review*, *Chautauqua Literary Journal*, *Spillway*, *North Dakota Quarterly*, *Blue Fifth Review*, etc. In addition to poetry, he has published 2 novels, *Time Sharing* and *Faith in What?*, a story collection, *And Fools of God*, and 4 plays. He has been awarded fellowships from the National Endowment for the Arts, the NC Arts Council(twice), and the Pennsylvania Council on the Arts. He teaches Beginning, Intermediate, and Advanced online Fiction Writing for UNC Chapel Hill, for which he won their Excellence in Teaching Award in 2009. He is founder of Jacar Press, a Community Active publishing company. www.jacarpress.com. He has worked extensively with people in homeless shelters, women's shelters, prisons, literacy classes, and community sites, teaching writing.

Rustin Larson's poetry has appeared in *The New Yorker*, *The Iowa Review*, *North American Review*, *Poetry East*, and *The American Entomologist Poet's Guide to the Orders of Insects*. He is the author of *The Wine-Dark House* (Blue Light Press, 2009) and *Crazy Star* (selected for the Loess Hills Book's Poetry Series in 2005) and *Bum Cantos, Winter Jazz, & The Collected Discography of Morning*, winner of the 2013 Blue Light Book Award (Blue Light Press, San Francisco). A new book, *The Philosopher Savant*, is available from Glass Lyre Press.

Sean Lause teaches courses in Shakespeare, Literature and the Hero and Medical Ethics at Rhodes State College in Lima, Ohio. His poems have appeared in *The Minnesota Review*, *The Alaska Quarterly*, *Another Chicago Magazine*, *The Beloit Poetry Journal*, *The Pedestal*, *European Judaism*, *Sanskrit*,

Atlanta Review and *Poetry International*. His first book of poems, *Bestiary of Souls*, was published in 2013 by FutureCycle Press.

Helen Losse is the author of six collections of poetry, including *Facing a Lonely West, Mansion of Memory, Seriously Dangerous*, and *Better With Friends*. Her poems have been anthologized in *Literary Trails of the North Carolina Piedmont*, and are forthcoming in *The Southern Poetry Anthology, Volume VII: North Carolina*, and *Kakalak 2014*. The former Poetry Editor of *The Dead Mule School of Southern Literature*, she is an Associate Editor for *Kentucky Review*.

Ken Meisel is a poet and psychotherapist from the Detroit area. He is the author of five books of poetry, the most recent being *Scrap Metal Mantra Poems*, a finalist in the Main Street Rag Chapbook Contest, published in 2013 and *Beautiful Rust*, [Bottom Dog Press: 2009]. He is a 2012 Kresge Arts Literary Fellow and a Pushcart Prize nominee. His poems have been published in *Cream City Review, Rattle, San Pedro River Review, Boxcar Review, Birdfeast, Chaffin Journal* and *Concho River Review*.

Corey Mesler has published in numerous journals and anthologies. He has published 8 novels, 4 full length poetry collections, and 3 books of short stories. He has also published a dozen chapbooks of both poetry and prose. He has been nominated for the Pushcart Prize numerous times, and two of his poems were chosen for Garrison Keillor's *Writer's Almanac*. His fiction has received praise from John Grisham, Robert Olen Butler, Lee Smith, Frederick Barthelme, Greil Marcus, among others. With his wife, he runs Burke's Book Store in Memphis, TN. He can be found at www.coreymesler.wordpress.com.

Naila Moreira works at Smith College as a writing instructor at the Jacobson Writing Center and a lecturer in the English department. Her journalism and nature writing has been published in *The Boston Globe, The Seattle Times, Science News, The Common Online*, and other venues.

Anne Britting Oleson has been published widely in North America, Europe and Asia. She earned her MFA at the Stonecoast program of USM. She has published two chapbooks, *The Church of St. Materiana* (2007) and *The Beauty of It* (2010).

M. Nasorri Pavone is a graduate of the English Literature and Creative Writing Program at the University of California, Los Angeles. His poems have appeared in *The Cortland Review, La Fovea, Bluestem, Mudfish, New Letters, Harpur Palate, Stirring, Green Hills Literary Lantern, Main Street Rag, DMQ Review, Tiger's Eye, Quercus Review* and elsewhere, with work in the current *River Styx* and upcoming in *Quiddity, Packingtown Review* and *The Midwest Quarterly*. His first manuscript, *On the Wrong Bird* was selected as a semifinalist for the Blue Lynx Prize and as a finalist for the White Pine Press Poetry Prize. He is also a script analyst and playwright. His play *Feeding Time* celebrated its world premiere at the Hollywood Fringe Festival.

Jonathan K. Rice is editor/publisher of *Iodine Poetry Journal*. He is the author of *Shooting Pool With A Cellist* (Main Street Rag, 2003) and *Ukulele and Other Poems* (Main Street Rag, 2006). He is the recipient of the 2012 Irene Blair Honeycutt Legacy Award for outstanding service in support of local and regional writers, awarded by Central Piedmont Community College. He lives in Charlotte, NC with his family.

Val Dering Rojas is a Los Angeles based poet and artist. She is the author of the chapbook *TEN* (2014, Dancing Girl Press), and her poetry and short fiction has been included in *Referential Magazine, Dogzplot, Crack the Spine*, and *Right Hand Pointing*, among others.

Judith Skillman's how-to is *Broken Lines—The Art & Craft of Poetry*, from Lummox Press. Poems have appeared in *Poetry, FIELD, Seneca Review, The Iowa Review, Southern Review, Pontoon*, and other journals and anthologies. Skillman is the recipient of an Eric Mathieu King Fund Award from the Academy of American Poets for Storm, Blue Begonia Press. She has taught at City University, Richard Hugo House, and elsewhere. *Angles of Separation*, her new book, is available from Glass Lyre Press. Also visit judithskillman.com.

Joannie Stangeland is the author of *In Both Hands* and *Into the Rumored Spring*, both published by Ravenna Press, and two chapbooks. Her poems have also appeared in *Clockhouse, Off the Coast, Valparaiso Poetry Review*, and other journals. Joannie works as a technical writer and helps out at the family winery.

Annie Stenzel's poems have most recently appeared in the print journals *Catamaran Literary Reader, Quiddity* and *Sow's Ear Poetry Review*; in anthologies titled *Patient Poets* and *Ten Years of Medicine and the Arts*; and in the online journal *Unsplendid*. She has work forthcoming in *Lunch Ticket* and in the British journal, *Ambit*. She is also a letterpress printer, and was a member of a Bay Area collective called Thicket Press, which published a number of hand-bound chapbooks and broadsides. She pays the bills by working at a mid-sized law firm in San Francisco.

Maria Terrone is the author of the poetry collections *Eye to Eye* (Bordighera Press, 2014); *A Secret Room in Fall* (McGovern Prize, Ashland Poetry Press) and *The Bodies We Were Loaned* (The Word Works), as well as a chapbook *American Gothic, Take 2* (Finishing Line Press). Her work, which has been published in French and Farsi and nominated four times for a Pushcart Prize, has appeared in magazines including *Poetry, Ploughshares, The Hudson Review,* and *Poetry International* and in more than 20 anthologies. She was one of 10 Queens-based authors commissioned by the Guggenheim Museum to write an essay for its performance project, "stillspotting nyc" and was a fellow this year at the Virginia Center for the Creative Arts. Visit her at www.mariaterrone.com

Donna Vorreyer is the author of *A House of Many Windows* (Sundress Publications, 2013). Her work has appeared in many journals including *RHINO, Linebreak, Cider Press Review, Stirring, Sweet, wicked alice*, and *Weave*. Her fifth chapbook, *We Build Houses of Our Bodies* was released in late 2013 by Dancing Girl Press, and her second poetry collection is forthcoming from Sundress Publications in 2016.

Martin Willitts Jr. is a retired Librarian. He won the International Dylan Thomas Poetry Award for the centennial. He has 28 chapbooks and 10 full-length collections, including national ecological winner, *Searching For What Is Not There*. His forthcoming collections include *How to Be Silent* (FutureCycle Press) and *Irises, the Lightning Conductor of Van Gogh's Illness* (Aldrich Press). His poems have appeared in *Kentucky Review, Comstock Review, Nine Mile, Stone Canoe, Bitter Oleander, Red Poppy Review, Centrifugal Eye,* and others.

Nancy Wilson is a lifetime resident of Chicago who currently resides in Des Plaines, Illinois. She is a semi-retired phebotomist and lab technician (she's the one that takes your blood bwaaaaaa) and is a lover of all things British. She collects Beatle memorabilia, loves music and film and traveled for her first time across the pond in 2014 to celebrate the 50 year anniversary of the Fab Four!

Sarah Ann Winn lives in Virginia. Her poems have appeared or will appear in *Day One, Cider Press Review, Massachusetts Review, Quarterly West*, and *RHINO*, among others. Her chapbook, *Portage*, was released by Sundress Publications in February 2015. Visit her at http://bluebirdwords.com or follow her @blueaisling on Twitter.

Bill Yarrow is the author of *The Lice of Christ* (MadHat Press, 2014), *Incompetent Translations and Inept Haiku* (Červená Barva Press, 2013) and *Pointed Sentences* (BlazeVOX, 2012). His poems have appeared in many print and online magazines including *Poetry International, RHINO, Contrary, DIAGRAM, Gargoyle, THRUSH Poetry Journal*, and *PANK*. He is a Professor of English at Joliet Junior College where he teaches creative writing, Shakespeare, and film.

"Ever since *Leaves of Grass* first appeared in 1855, we find Walt Whitman simultaneously falsely imitated and truly manifesting in America. Who would have thought that his latest local incarnation would be in the body and the soul of an exceptional woman born in Gaya, Bihar, India, where the Buddha experienced Enlightenment? Yet here he is..."

— Jack Foley

the Selected Poems series

Our Selected Poems series highlights contemporary poets with a substantial body of published work to their credit. Our goal is to resurrect superb but often out-of-print poems.

the Good Works projects

Our Good Works projects are thematic anthologies of individual works devoted to significant issues affecting our world. All proceeds from sales are donated to charities.

Visit us for info, catalog, and submission guidelines

futurecycle.org

Free Kindle Saturdays and countdown deals

Check our Catalog tab each Saturday

Monthly Goodreads Giveaways

Book excerpts in our Goodreads group

Crazy Star

POEMS BY
RUSTIN LARSON

MIDWESTERN GOTHIC
A LITERARY JOURNAL

Midwestern Gothic aims to collect the very best in Midwestern fiction writing in a way that has never been done before, cataloging the oeuvre of an often overlooked region of the United States ripe with its own mythologies and tall tales.

$12 PRINT
$2.99 EBOOK

SUBSCRIPTIONS
1 YEAR / 4 ISSUES
$40 PRINT / $10 EBOOK

MIDWESTGOTHIC.COM
FOLLOW US ON TWITTER @MWGOTHIC

Glass Lyre Press

exceptional works to replenish the spirit

Glass Lyre Press is an independent literary publisher interested in technically accomplished, stylistically distinct, and original work. Glass Lyre seeks diverse writers that possess a dynamic aesthetic, and an ability to emotionally and intellectually engage a wide audience of readers.

Glass Lyre's vision is to connect the world through language and art. We hope to expand the scope of poetry and short fiction for the general reader through exceptionally well-written books, which evoke emotion, provide insight, and resonate with the human spirit.

Poetry Collections
Poetry Chapbooks
Select Short & Flash Fiction
Anthologies

www.GlassLyrePress.com